*You too can*
# BECOME A SUCCESS

HELEN ORITSEJAFOR

You Too Can Become A Success

Copyright © 2020 by Helen Oritsejafor

Published by:
Word Alive Productions
P.O Box 2088, Warri Delta State, Nigeria.
Tel: 07061640469, 08126288633
E-mail: mamahelen@ayo-oritsejafor.org

*No portion of this publication may be translated into any language or reproduced in any form, except for brief quotations in reviews, without written permission of the author and publisher.*

Printed in Nigeria
Benco Color Media Ltd.
+234 803 718 5466
www.bencocolormedia.com

# Content

DEDICATION

ACKNOWLEDGMENT

INTRODUCTION

**CHAPTER ONE**
## SUCCESS ........................................... 1

**CHAPTER TWO**
## FAMINE ............................................ 29

**CHAPTER THREE**
## SUCCESS NEEDS ............................. 45

**CHAPTER FOUR**
## STRATEGIES TO SUCCEED ............. 59

**CHAPTER FIVE**
## THE PATH TO SUCCESS ................... 81

**CHAPTER SIX**
## SUCCESS IN BUSINESS ................... 95

**CHAPTER SEVEN**
## STRATEGIES TO ATTAIN SUCCESS THROUGH BIBLICAL EXAMPLES ........................ 109

**CHAPTER EIGHT**
## USING WHAT YOU HAVE TO ACHIEVE SUCCESS ......... 127

**CHAPTER NINE**
**FROM SUCCESS
TO GREATNESS (I)** _137_

**CHAPTER TEN**
**FROM SUCCESS
TO GREATNESS (II)** _165_

**CHAPTER ELEVEN**
**THE SUPERNATURAL
PATH TO GREATNESS** _177_

**NOTE FROM THE AUTHOR** _192_

# Dedication

To everyone who is determined to break all limits with the conviction that they are indeed capable to succeed.

# Introduction

Many people think that there are certain people who are destined to succeed and be great from birth. But is this truly the case? Is success so impossible to achieve? Is it so difficult to succeed in whatever we do? These are the burning questions that this book provides answers for.

According to Jeremiah 29:11;

*'For I know the thoughts that I think toward you, saith the LORD, thoughts of peace, and not of evil, to give you an expected end'.*

Scripturally, God did not bring us into the world to fail. He brought every human being to earth to be successful. But overtime, humans dwelt solely on the word without backing it up with actions, which eventually led to failure.

Hard work will make your goal and desire achievable. But to enjoy the euphoria of everlasting success, a wonderful relationship with God Almighty combined with working hard is of great necessity.

The right mind set, the zeal to pay the price, the enthusiasm to fight till the very end, and to rise no matter how many times you hit rock bottom should always reside on the inside because failure on the path to success is inevitable.

So, to become a success story, it is necessary to imbibe the spirit of determination and the attitude of perseverance irrespective of negative outcomes.

As children of God, we are not just brought into this world to be successful, we are also meant to bask in greatness, it is our right for it to be that way.

This book opens our understanding and explores the concept of success in terms of its requirements, the relationships necessary to meet those needs, the strategies that need to be made, and the path through which success can be transformed into greatness.

So, allow me to transport your mind spiritually, mentally, physically, and emotionally into the unending realm of success and greatness.

Be prepared to break out of that status quo and leap to the height which God has rightly destined for you to be.

# CHAPTER ONE
## SUCCESS

> 'Success is not final, failure is not fatal, what counts is our ability to keep going.'

CHAPTER ONE

# SUCCESS

Before I define what success is, it is important to know what it is not. Success is not the absence of challenges, neither is it undertaking actions just for the fun of it.

Instead, success is the ability to accomplish a task. It is neither magical nor mysterious. It is the natural consequence of consistently applying the fundamentals necessary for the quest. It is the favourable outcome of a goal, aim, or purpose. It is also the ability to put in the required effort and to experience success. My last statement is important because carrying out the action is not enough to determine success; the outcome is also important.

Success is the cumulation of doing something and it's resultant effect.

In learning about success, it is also important to know that *'Success is not final, failure is not fatal, what counts is our ability to keep going.'*

"Success is not final" implies that you must be determined to continue moving up the ladder of success until death comes. For instance, a man decides to embark on a journey, he buys his ticket, and gets his visa. Although getting those two travel requirements are important, he is not yet at the end of that success story until he embarks on the journey and perhaps, achieves his aim for the journey.

When I say: "Failure is not fatal," I mean that one must be determined to never give up despite the trials and tribulations they may face. So, if you are going through a difficult situation right now, smile because it is only temporary; prepare to become an overcomer soon.

Probably you find it difficult to understand your spouse right now, do not give up, it is only temporary. Or maybe, business seems to be shaky at the moment and you are wondering how long it will be that way; I want to let you know that it is a temporary situation.

*"It is not of he that willeth or runneth, but it is the Lord that showeth mercy"*
*Romans 9:16(KJV)*

Pastor Ayo Oritsejafor, who is a success story, has gone through many hurdles, but he has always overcome them through the help of God. This same God will pull you out of those pressing situations. That difficult moment is coming to an end, in the name of Jesus.

It is the will of God that we should prosper, however we must not be ignorant of the fact that there will be challenges, trials, and some difficult times. The uniqueness of the journey, is the experience and the eventual success.
No matter what you might be going through, once you embrace and practice the Spirit of faith, you are bound to be on a more stable path to success. No condition or person will be able to stop you from reaching your full potential when God has created a path for you.

Will there be times when things may not work out the way we planned? Yes! Am I saying that as a Christian you would not experience failure? Of course not.
Even in difficult times, you can always guarantee that success will be yours when walking in accordance to His will.

## When God's Work was Interrupted

In the book of Genesis chapter one, the Bible makes us understand that God created the heavens and the earth. However, there was an interruption. Darkness covered the face of the earth.
In *verse 3; "God said let there be light: and there was light"*, and He continued from where He left off.

If God also had His fair share of delay but yet endured, and continued with the plans He had, then who are we not to follow the footsteps of the Father?

With God, it can never be too late!

God wants every one of His children to succeed on earth. He has mapped out a plan for our progress in life. Confess with your mouth that you are a success story. Whatever has stopped you in life, I challenge that foundation now and declare you free, in the name of Jesus. Who can stop God? If no one is capable of that, then the same thing applies to His children. I release the blood of Jesus over your job, children, husband, wife. I decree and declare, Satan touch not, in the name of Jesus.

As the children of God walked around the wall of Jericho until it fell, so also every wall of Jericho that has prevented you from going into every plan God has mapped out for you, will fall in Jesus' name.

## HINDRANCES TO SUCCESS

It is inevitable to experience hindrances on the road to success. These hindrances which can either make or mar a person include:

### 1.) Hurt

The voice of hurt may not be obvious to others, but it is the loudest voice for the person experiencing it.

It can be related to the initial stages of a person's life and could happen in so many ways.

For instance, some people have experienced a series of abusive relationships that have ruined their perspective on marital bliss. While others may carry a constant reminder of something as hurtful as childhood abuse.

A protégée of mine once said to me, "Mama, I do not want to get married!" I was amazed at her stance. She was well mannered and educated. But I later found out that she made that decision because of past heartbreaks.

God will not disappoint you the way men do. He does not break hearts; rather he mends broken hearts. A man may fail you, but God has something special planned out for your life.

Some people need to pull out of that state of depression and self-pity and allow themselves to be healed of that pain. God permits us to go through challenges for a reason and eventually come out as overcomers.

*"For his anger endureth but a moment; in his favour is life: weeping may endure for a night, but joy comes in the morning."*
*Psalm 30:5(KJV)*

I see the joy of the Lord resting upon every one of His children. Therefore, every attempt made from now will result in success in the name of Jesus.
I recognize the fact that you have gone through difficult times, but all will be well. Forgive yourself and your offenders and receive the love of God.

## 2.) Past Failure

*"For a just man falleth seven times, and riseth up again: but the wicked shall fall into mischief."*
*Proverbs 24:16(KJV)*

*"Rejoice not against me, O mine enemy: when I fall, I shall arise: when I sit in darkness, the LORD shall be a light unto me." Micah 7:8(KJV)*

The fact that the business collapsed is not the end of the world!

Thomas Edison is a great inspiration in this regard. He attempted to create electricity and failed nine hundred and ninety-nine times. When a journalist asked him about it, he said 'I did not fail all those times, I have only learnt in nine hundred and ninety-nine times how not to produce electricity.'

One of the ways by which failure can be overcome is to learn from past experiences. To do that, one must be willing to:

### a) Bebold enough to admit the truth:

That is, being determined to realize what led to that failure. Embrace reality, no matter how harsh it may be. Note that spiritual factors should also be considered.

### b) Do a personal re-evaluation:

Is it alright to try and fail? yes!

Ask yourself questions like; "What am I doing wrong?" "Do I know how to maintain relationships?" "Am I a faithful person towards my business and life?"

It is popular in our clime to find men and women who think that the first course of a business is all about their personal and immediate needs. Due to this fallacy, they are

swift to cheat people and ruin relationships. When you become more enlightened, you would realize that the continuity of your business is important.
When you only think about immediate profit, you rob yourself of future profit.

On the path to success, failure is inevitable. Endeavour to keep putting in the effort and never give up, no matter the situation or circumstance. In the end, you will succeed.

One thing that has helped me through the years is that I refuse to give up when I am going through challenges .That is why my chain of businesses are still growing. Whatever it is that you are going through, someone else has gone through it and come out of it victoriously. God will bring you out of the challenge you are currently facing. He will give you the wisdom to navigate your way out of that problem in Jesus' name.

### c.) Do not apportion blames to others
Do not be quick to blame others for the challenges in your life. Some people blame their parent's lineage or background. Although these could be genuine reasons, learn to focus more on what you can do as a person to achieve better results.

### 3.) Fear
The very first place where the devil captures his victims is in the mind. He takes over their thought patterns.

It has been scientifically proven that ninety percent of what people are afraid of never happen. It has also been proven that ninety-nine percent of our thought patterns are not our thoughts. Rather, they come into our minds after we hear or see something from an external source.

Thoughts produce fear when we dwell on it or give it supremacy over us.

Some people are afraid of flying because they fear there will be a plane crash. Do not allow your circumstances to determine the words that come out of your mouth.

I decree and declare today that whatever is bringing fear into your life will not last. I challenge that fear that you will not make it or that your business will go down. I decree and declare that you are free from that fear of failure and defeat, in Jesus' name.

Fear is an emotional display of our thoughts.

It is a thought pattern that creates events in the absence of none. It is an imaginary notion that occurs when negative thoughts are pondered upon.

*"Casting down imaginations and everything that exalts itself against the knowledge of God."*
*2Corinthians10:5(KJV).*

Whatever encourages fear is of the devil. Have you ever wondered why people have panic attacks? It is because they allow their minds to experience fear, which affects not only their minds but also their bodies. For such people, most times, the doctors are unable to diagnose an illness in their physical bodies.

I declare you free, in the name of Jesus.

Faith makes you succeed in the face of failure; it makes you a victor, not a victim. It makes you a winner ahead of time.

Fear should be scared of you!

In Matthew 14:24, *But the ship was now in the midst of the sea, tossed with waves: for the wind was contrary.* In other words, the wind was blowing against them. When the wind of life blows against you, you will be frustrated.

When the wind is contrary in a woman's life, she can experience a series of miscarriages in a year. When it is contrary in a business, in the same business that everyone makes a profit, it makes losses.

In verses 26-27; *And when the disciples saw Him walking on the sea, they were troubled, saying, it is a spirit, and they cried out for fear. But straightway Jesus spake unto them, saying, be of good cheer; it is I; be not afraid.*

As Peter stepped on the water that was the cause of their fear, you will step on whatever is the cause of fear in your life in the name of Jesus.

Fear can make you give what is rightfully yours to the enemy.

I challenge whatever it is that says you will not do better than where you are now or achieve more than you have already achieved, in the name of Jesus.

As children of God, we are meant to proclaim His word that says, *"by his stripes, we are healed."* The more we allow our thought to dwell on illness, the more the illness will persist.

Also, your dream patterns may be as a result of the state of your mind. For instance, if you always preoccupy yourself with thoughts of demonic activities, it would not be strange to have such experiences in your sleep.

I decree and declare that Satan will not have a hold over you.

If I am permitted to go in the Spirit and find out the kind of thoughts you're preoccupied with, what will I find? Thoughts of wickedness or evil? I decree today, that as led by the spirit of God, you will have control over your mind.

Remember that you are who God says you are. Endeavour to ponder on that at all times.

You must learn to properly deal with wrong thoughts. Do not allow it to dominate your mind.

As Christians, we cannot live a better life if we do not change our thought patterns.
Satan has no power unless you empower him, that is why the Bible says in
Proverbs 23:7; "*As a man thinketh in his heart, so is he*".

For instance, I do not believe anyone can kill me. They can try, but will never succeed. You are supposed to think and speak that way when you know who you are and whom you carry within. Also, the presence of the Holy Spirit within is a guarantee that you cannot be ruled by satanic oppressions or marine forces.

In Jeremiah 1:6, Jeremiah found it difficult to believe

all that God had assigned to him. His response? *"Ah, Lord GOD! behold I cannot speak: for I am a child"*. Fear triggered his response, thereby taking away his boldness and self-worth.

The spirit of fear welcomes what God did not originally visualize for our lives. Today, many people have committed suicide because of their thought patterns.

I decree that anything that has made you feel small or made you lose faith in yourself; you will overcome, in the name of Jesus.

The Bible makes us understand that before Jeremiah made that statement in verse 6, God said to him, in *verse 5, "Before I formed thee in the belly I knew thee; and before thou camest forth out of the womb I sanctified thee, and I ordained thee a prophet unto the nations" (KJV)*.

What God was implying here was, that He had already plotted out a graph for Jeremiah's life before he came into existence. So, he was not to be overthrown. He was, therefore, not to look at himself as merely a child, but as who God had declared him to be. God had worked on him without his knowledge and had empowered him far beyond his expectations.

In order for it to be actualised, God commanded that the prophet dig into his mind; overcome his thoughts, and get rid of all imaginations that had enslaved him.

God is saying to someone *"the thoughts I have towards you are thoughts of good and not of evil"*. Therefore, replace your thoughts with better thoughts and go out to be who He has ordained you to be on earth.

**4.) Regret**

We all have regrets in life. While some regret getting married to their present spouses, others have regrets about the decisions they made in the past. The voice of regret has enslaved a lot of people; it has put them in stagnancy.

Regret hinders us from enhancing our abilities!

But I speak to someone reading this; whatever it is that has led to regret, whether from the past or present, thank God for who and what you are now. Let go of the regret harboured in the inside. Get over it and move on.
Endeavour to make the best out of every decision made!

In the area of marriage, husband, remember your wife was your choice, so, celebrate her. Even if she was chosen for you, choose to love her, and the same goes for the wives.

As an individual, choose not to let another's perception of you be the definition of who you are.

You are who God says you are!

You carry God on the inside, and He died for you. You are worth the blood of Jesus. Let that be your identity.

.

**5.) Pride**

A proud man cannot be taught because he comes to the table with the assumption that he knows it all.

Do not work with people with the assumption that you already know everything.

Pride goeth before a fall!

Proud people are unteachable, uncorrectable, and cannot be directed.

*"But he giveth more grace. Wherefore he saith, God resisteth the proud, but giveth grace unto the humble."*
*James 4:6(KJV)*

To resist means to forcefully stop something or someone from making progress.

If God is against you, then you are finished.

## 6) Carelessness

Many people are careless about how they deal with things in their lives.

Careless people do not follow the rules. They do things haphazardly without thinking of what the repercussions might be. They do not pay much attention to the details. Due to their attitude and their way of life, they tend to lose opportunities or responsibilities given to them. They also lose credibility before others.

## 7.) Disappointment

Most of the time fear causes anxiety, which in turn will yield disappointment.

God has given us the power to tread upon them. No marine spirit should be permitted to put you under.

God desires for us to be on top because we are destined to win.

### Overcoming Disappointment

*"There hath no temptation taken you but such as is common to man: but God is faithful, who will not suffer you to be tempted above that ye are able; but will with the temptation also make a way to escape, that ye may be able to bear it."*

1Corinthians10:13(KJV)

From the above scripture, we see God's intention and pronouncement concerning this hindrance. We can deduce that He is saying we should adhere to His word which says:

- Stop the assumption that your problem is the biggest and greatest in the world. Whenever trouble rears its ugly head, the devil tries to infiltrate such ideas.

- Remember that God is ever faithful. The God you believe, is forever reliable and trustworthy in all situations of life. The Lord your God is indeed God, and He is the faithful one that keeps His covenant with them that love Him.

*"Let us hold fast the profession of our faith without wavering; (for He is faithful that promised)."* Hebrews10:23(KJV)

- God already knows you can overcome any problem. That means that any temptation that comes to you, you will defeat it. He has a standing rule. He will not permit any temptation to come to your life without the corresponding knowledge that you need to overcome it.

- Rejoice always. You are to do this not because you are experiencing a challenge but because you know God has put the power within you to overcome it.
- Believe and understand that there is a way of escape. Each morning, tell the devil, "God has made a way of escape for me".

When that business is not going well, or things in your life are not going as planned, repeat the words "God has made a way of escape for me."

*"And thine ears shall hear a word behind thee, saying, this is the way, walk ye in it, when ye turn to the right hand, and when ye turn to the left."* Isaiah 30:21(KJV)

When you know that God has made a way, all you need to do is begin to look for the way!

*"And I will bring the blind by a way that they knew not; I will lead them in paths that they have not known: I will make darkness light before them, and crooked things straight. These things will I do unto them, and not forsake them."*

*Isaiah 42:16(KJV)*

*"The Lord knoweth how to deliver the godly out of temptations, and to reserve the unjust unto the day of judgment to be punished."*

*2 Peter 2:9(KJV)*

There is a way of escape! God has already made that

way possible. Your disappointment will become an appointment. As you believe in the word of God, you will begin to see the way of escape.

### 8.) Foolishness

From various perspectives, foolishness can be defined in various forms:

- It is the inability of not making use of one's common sense
- It is the failure to generate ideas that will make a business prosperous. It is better to make a foolish decision than not to make one at all. A man who finds it difficult to make decisions is worse than foolishness itself.

I decree and declare that every wrong decision you have made, will be worked out by God and turned to good.

The Bible referred to the foolish virgins as people who could not think.

Thinkers are achievers, achievers are thinkers!

Good things do not just happen, someone must think and come up with ideas that will put food on the table.

Gone are the days when you expect manna to fall from heaven. God is now teaching men how to fish.

- Foolishness is hiring an insignificant head in an organization, simply out of emotions.

| SUCCESS |

A lot of companies are facing challenges today, because, they want to help family members or relatives. That is foolishness. The money you need to invest in that business is wasted on those who have no intention to add value to you. It is only a fool who will sit at home, fast and pray day and night, believing God to get a job without applying for one.

The book of James chapter 5 says *"faith without works is dead"*.

- Foolishness is when a thirty-year-old woman dresses like an elderly woman, while still expecting God to bless her with a husband.

Good judgement should tell you that since you are still expectant of a husband, you should package yourself. Whether you speak in tongues for a hundred days, a man still has to look and be attracted first. So, if there is nothing attractive to find in you, why should anyone pay attention? Some ladies become so holy that they neglect their appearance and become less attractive. Their skirts are extremely long. Their shoes bent, even their mouths smell.

In the book of 1 Samuel, a foolish boy was to govern a country. The people asked him how he was going to rule. Requesting for time, he went to the elders who told him to treat the people well. He, however, inquired from his peers who gave him contrary advice. In the end, he took the advice of his peers, and everyone had to live with the consequences of his decision.

When a man refuses wisdom, his food becomes sand. May that not be your portion in the name of Jesus.

The foolish virgins did not prepare. Foolishness will make you unprepared.

The Bible says they were foolish, they thought that the master will come on time, but he was delayed. The lamps they carried dried up, and they had no spare oil. At midnight, he arrived, but their lamps had gone off. They then asked for some oil from the wise virgins who did not have to spare.

Wealth does not grow magically; people intentionally make it to grow!

You can start from little, and in no time, wealth will begin to grow in your hands.

If you are the kind of person who spends whatever amount of money you get; then nothing good will come out of you.

The great men and women you see and hear of today learnt how to save.

The foolish virgins did not save. When the time of necessity came, they missed it. But those who were wise and ready entered and shut the door.

May the door of opportunity, increase, success, greatness never be shut against you in the name of Jesus.

**9) Weakness.**

*"I know thy works: behold, I have set before thee an open door, and no man can shut it: for thou hast a little strength, and hast kept my word, and hast not denied my name."*

*Revelation 3:8(KJV)*

What and who has weakened you? what is it that has prevented you from entering? Today, I challenge every power that has brought weakness into your life; marriage, business, joy. I come against it by the voice of Jehovah in the name of Jesus. Take your strength back in the name of Jesus.

In the book of 1 Samuel 1 and 2, the Bible tells us about Hannah and Peninnah. Peninnah continuously made a jest of Hannah, because she had no child.

What are those areas of weakness that people see in you that cause them to laugh at you? God says to tell you that He will reply on your behalf in the name of Jesus.

Hannah was weak to a point because she saw Peninnah who was competing with her, bearing children with ease.

Life may have defeated you; it may have given you blows which has made you begin to doubt God, but I declare to you, whatsoever will give you your strength, take it, in the name of Jesus.

Whenever Hannah saw Peninnah she would hide. Are there things in your life that have made you hide whenever your friends come around? Probably because you do not have children yet, or because you have been out of work for a long time and you do not want them to ask you questions?

But a time came when she could not take it anymore, and she went to Shiloh to meet with God. She cried unto the Lord, and He answered her.

The story of her life changed from then on; she became a mother of five children.

I prophesy upon your life that whatever has taken away your strength, will come back to you double. In your marriage receive double, in your business receive double, in your destiny receive double in the name of Jesus.

In 2kings 18:13, we read about a king by the name Sennacherib, king of Syria, who decided to wage war against the children of Israel. Hezekiah who was the King of Israel then, did everything possible to save the people. The Bible says out of fear, Hezekiah stripped the house of God of everything valuable and gave them to the King of Syria. You cannot bribe your enemies; it is a waste of time. The more you give to them, the more they take and the more they despise you.

When you sit to discuss business, you do not go in weak.

If you do, they will see through you, and they will negotiate you out. But when you go in with strength and vigour, and tell them how it will be, they perceive that you know what you are talking about. Do not sell out. What you carry inside is greater. It is not about your physique or background, it is about Christ in you, the hope of glory. David did not kill Goliath by his size or strength, it was all because of the Lord. God is here today to fight your battles.

Anything challenging your beginning, God will destroy in the name of Jesus.

In verse 3, Hezekiah gave his servant a message to take to Isaiah.

*"And they said unto him, thus saith Hezekiah, this day is a day of trouble, and rebuke, and blasphemy: for the children have come to the birth, and there is not strength to bring forth." 2 Kings 19:3(KJV)*

Isaiah sent the servant back with a word in verse 6,

*"And Isaiah said unto them, thus shall ye say to your master, thus saith the LORD, be not afraid of the words which thou hast heard, with which the servants of the king of Assyria have blasphemed me."*

God said, Hezekiah, this battle is not yours but the Lords!

Every battle in your marriage; confronting your children, raging against your business or job, the Lord will fight it for you.

## 10.) The Gate (Spiritual Warfare)

The word gate means to be limited.

It means for someone to put a stop to your life, destiny, or growth.

Like a man or woman who intends to step into a realm, and someone is restricting him or her from doing so. Every restriction in your life shall be lifted, in the name of Jesus.

Anything that has brought limitation to your life, it shall be lifted now, in the name of Jesus. In your body it will be lifted, in your marriage, it will be lifted, on the job it will be lifted, in the name of Jesus.

Who is that person that says you will not arrive at your destination? Who says you will not have children? Who is that man or woman standing at the gate of your success? I decree and declare that whosoever stands against your success; growth, advancement, breakthroughs, your ability to have children, against your destiny, will crumble today, in the name of Jesus.

Hannah possessed the gate of her enemies when she became a mother.

Peninnah thought her case was over, but God showed to Peninnah that He had not forgotten Hannah.
Sarah thought her story of childbirth will never come, until God intervened, and empowered her to possess the gates of her enemies.

I do not know where you are right now. It may have tarried for too long. But God will have me tell you that as Sarah was able to possess the gates of her enemies, so also will you, in the name of Jesus.

What they said you could not have; you will have it,

where they said you could not get to, you will get there, in the name of Jesus.

*"Command therefore that the sepulchre is made sure until the third day, lest his disciples come by night, and steal him away, and say unto the people, He has risen from the dead: so, the last error shall be worse than the first. Pilate said unto them, Ye have a watch: go your way, make it as sure as ye can"*, Matthew 27:64-65(KJV)

There are gatekeepers; monitoring agents, who may be physical or spiritual.

The spiritual ones take the battle to the spirit realm and begin to fight, while the physical ones do it in the physical. They plot against you; tell lies against you, and do anything possible to destroy your name. But God says to tell you that any conspiracy against you shall never stand. Whether it is at your place of work; against your marriage, children, business, I command them to fall right before you.

The Bible says *"The evil bow before the good; and the wicked at the gates of the righteous"* Proverbs 14:19 (KJV).

Anything they said you will never have, you will have them, in the name of Jesus. Take your victory, joy, laughter in the name of Jesus.

Who are those troubling you? God sent me on an errand to tell you, He will trouble them, in the name of Jesus.

Whosoever is fighting you; I will fight them, whosoever is stopping you, I will stop them, whoever says you will not succeed they will fail, in the name of Jesus.

They wanted to intentionally stop Jesus from rising. They knew that if He arose; it will bring healing, salvation, deliverance, success, and promotion to man. Satan knew and did all he could to prevent Jesus from rising.

Although the enemy might have planned to stop you, God has planned your escape, in the name of Jesus.

You will escape from that trap; sickness, trial, affliction, everyone and anything trying to stop you, in the name of Jesus.

They did not only form a guard over his tomb, but they also sealed it with stone.

There are times the enemy thinks he has won the battle, but God always surprises them.

Whoever is monitoring your business; I command them to collapse, whoever is monitoring your home, I command them to be blinded and be put to shame in the name of Jesus.

There are different kinds of gates: the gate of barrenness, poverty, sickness and affliction, almost there-syndrome, the gate against marriages, the gate of rising and falling, etc.

Whatever is at the gate of your breakthrough, will be consumed by the fire of the Holy Ghost, in the name of Jesus.

In dealing with the battle at the gate, there are two enemies that can try to stop your elevation:

- **The Enemy of Your Life**

The enemy of your life needs your permission to stop you!

Do not surrender to your enemy. Do not give the enemy permission to stop your job, career, joy, and destiny.

Businesses fail when bad decisions override good judgement. Marriages hit the rock when couples start taking each other for granted. You step out of grace when you begin to look down, instead of upwards to who God has placed over you.

You surrender your destiny to the enemy when you refuse to do anything about it. You lose your money when you refuse to invest wisely. You cease to move to the next level at the place of work because you refuse to do what will make you move to the next level.

Do not give power to the enemy. The strength of the ministry gets reduced when we start fighting ourselves instead of the enemy at the gate. The promotion you are looking for has already left heaven, all you need to do is to improve your self well enough, to be able to occupy that position.

Joseph had to go through training because God knew where He was taking him to. He knew that if he went there with that small mind of his, he would miss it. So, He had to let him go through the pit and prison experience, for him to reign in the palace.

There are some of us going through either of these experiences, but God says to tell you that it is all over.

According to Psalm 30:5, your joy has come, your laughter has come, in the name of Jesus.

- **The Enemy of Yourself (You)**

In the Book of Matthew chapter 28, the Bible made us understand that while the gatekeepers were rejoicing, something happened.

*"And behold, there was a great earthquake for the angel of the Lord descended from heaven and came and rolled back the stone from the door".*
Matthew 28:2(KJV)

They were celebrating, thinking that they had won. They thought they had stopped Him, but little did they know they had just given Him an incentive to move to the next level.

They think they have taken food from your mouth; they do not know that God set a table before you in the presence of your enemies.

They do not know you have just started a new thing. Where they left you, they will not find you there, in the name of Jesus.

What Must You Possess to Open All Gates?
There are two things you must have to be able to open gates:

- **Hope**

Most people think this is not necessary for the life of a believer. It is hope that keeps faith alive. Without it, you cannot exercise anything. If you lack something to hope for, your faith will not have substance.

Hope is what you have not seen but believe will occur.

- **Faith**

In the Book of Luke chapter 8, the Bible tells us about the woman with the issue of blood. She had carried that plague for twelve years. She was continuously bleeding, which made her smell, causing people to avoid her. But she believed that one day it would all be over.

The Bible says when she saw Jesus, she realized that was the day she was waiting for. So, she moved to press on to the garment of Jesus.

Her hope combined with her faith, caused her to get her healing.

If you have dropped your hope and faith, I am asking you to pick it up again.

Let your faith and hope come alive to receive what God has in store for you. You have waited for Him for too long, and you wonder if it will ever happen, God says to tell you that it will happen.

Your hope will not fail you; it will not embarrass you, in the name of Jesus. The fact that you are reading this book, is an indication that you have enough faith to believe your miracle and breakthrough is about to happen. Keep believing, do not let go of your faith and you will move to your next level.

## PRAYER

- In the name of Jesus, you spirit of fear, your time is up. I bind you and command you to come out in the name of Jesus.
- I cast down every imagination, every thought that exalts itself above what God says about me. I bring them into the obedience of Jesus, and I approve of what God says about me. I am who God says I am! I am a success!
- Every evil gatekeeper, today, I terminate your assignment in my life, in the life of my children, in the life of my spouse, concerning my business, my job, my education, my career, my advancement in the name of Jesus. I terminate your assignment, leave the church alone, leave our establishments alone, leave our children alone, in the name of Jesus.
- Father as you caused Jesus to rise from the grave, cause me to rise from my situation, from my predicament, from my limitation, from my obstacle, Oh Lord! cause me to rise.

CHAPTER TWO

# FAMINE

> In famine,
> he will redeem thee
> from death: and in war
> from the power
> of the sword.

CHAPTER TWO

# FAMINE

Famine implies a period of insufficiency or deprivation. It is a period of extreme lack and shortage of anything.

People can experience either financial, spiritual, or educational famine in life.

*"In famine, he will redeem thee from death: and in war from the power of the sword."*
*Job 5:20(KJV)*

*"At destruction and famine, thou shalt laugh: neither shalt thou be afraid of the beasts of the earth."*
*Job 5:22(KJV)*

From these scriptures, God assures us of comfort, protection, and peace of mind during the period of famine. He also promises to accommodate every problem that we may encounter along the way.

God told me to tell those who are going through the period of famine, that He has located that problem or situation and the days of famine are over. Every source of famine that has fought your growth, I put an end to it today in the name of Jesus.

I decree and declare that anything that is trying to destroy you is consumed by the fire of God in the name of Jesus.

**What Produces Famine?**

Economically, famine can develop from scarcity, inflation, or population disparity in a country. It can also be as a result of wrong policies or the carelessness of man.

Many times, when the United Nations or the Western world address the issues of famine; the first thing they think of is how to make food and clothing available. If it occurs during the time of war, temporary shelter is created for the people as well. That seems like a well thought out plan to help mitigate the level of famine, but nothing has been developed to completely eradicate the existence of famine.

The fact that there is temporary accommodation, provision of food and clothing does not put an end to the plague called famine.

Have you ever heard of vision 2020? It is a strategy to eradicate poverty globally.

The Former Minister of Finance in Nigeria, Dr. Mrs. Ngozi Okonjo-Iweala once made a statement I thought was profound. It was at a summit where she was asked to deliver a paper on solutions to poverty. She said: "We need to learn how to do old things in a new way," and immediately I agreed with that.

In the book of Genesis chapter 26, Isaac was faced with famine just like his father had faced it in Genesis chapter 12. His father dug a well during his time of famine, Isaac also dug his well.

It is presumed that when people are going through a period of famine, they are not to do a thing about it, they are to keep their hands folded and wait. But the period of famine is when one needs to go back and dig a well.

Why Isaac Succeeded During His Period of Famine (Isaac's Principle)

Despite the season of famine, Isaac sowed in the land and succeeded because he portrayed these traits:

- **Obedience**

In the book of Genesis 26:2; God instructed him not to leave. He had planned to go to Egypt to sow his seeds during the famine period, but God stopped him, and He did as he was instructed.

If you want to live a life where you can face any challenge and come out successfully, you must be willing to be obedient.

Give yourself wholeheartedly to God. Be willing to adhere to all instructions no matter how awkward or difficult they might be.

Instructions can also come from your spiritual parents. How many are willing to obey when they are given instructions? Are you willing to go the length to obey instructions?

*"Let no man deceive you with vain words: for because of these things cometh the wrath of God upon the children of disobedience." Ephesians 5:6(KJV).*

*"And having in a readiness to revenge all disobedience, when your obedience is fulfilled." 2 Corinthians 10:6(KJV).*
Sometimes obedience makes you look stupid.

- **Faith**

*"Sojourn in this land, and I will be with thee, and will bless thee; for unto thee, and unto thy seed, I will give all these countries, and I will perform the oath which I sware unto Abraham thy father".*
*Genesis 26:3(KJV)*

God told him to remain in the land, that He will be with him, and bless him there.

The worst thing a man can do is to think or believe they can succeed without God.

Isaac was a wise man, because he believed in what God told him. Faith is not in the way you think, it is simply what you know.

"What you know" is simply information that everyone has heard. But you understand it and are convinced within that indeed it is true.

Isaac sowed by faith in a barren land, he knew that under normal circumstances, it was not going to yield anything.

### How to Eradicate Famine
**a.) Be Innovative**
Repackage your business.

FAMINE

Come up with something new and make a difference!

It may be the same office, but a little splash of paint can make it new. You may be selling the same thing as your neighbour, but you can make your environment look more attractive.

Isaac dug the same well his father dug, but it produced something different for him.

*"And Isaac sowed in that land and received in the same year a hundredfold and the Lord blessed him."*
*Genesis 26:12(KJV)*

## b.) Do not give up

In the period of famine, Isaac sowed and reaped bountifully and the Lord prospered him. Why? Because he refused to give up.

In *verse 13, "And the man waxed great and went forward and grew until he became very great in the land of famine."*

He did not throw in the towel. He did not ponder on where he would start from, rather he sowed.

One of the things that we know about famine is that when it occurs, the soil dries up because of the absence of water. But Isaac stepped out in faith and decided to sow despite that condition.

Every time you make up your mind to do something new in life, get ready for the enemy because he will try to derail you. Whoever and whatsoever tries to distract you, or push you out of the way, is stopped today in the name of Jesus.

Success only comes to a man who refuses to give up. You must realize that anything good in life must be fought for.

### c.) **Be Confident**
*"Cast not away, therefore your confidence, which hath great recompense of reward."*
*Hebrews 10:35(KJV)*

God expects us to participate in the making of a miracle. He loves participators, not spectators.
Jesus is saying get involved, do not sit and wait for it to fall on your laps, do something. When there is no confidence in God, something goes wrong! Confidence in God is like the driving force behind your faith.

When you lose your confidence, you panic. Fear steps in and paralyses your faith. You become the hindrance to your success, miracle, or that spectacular thing God wants to do in your life.

The devil knows what you carry, that is why he will do anything and everything to take your confidence from you.
You cannot have confidence in someone you do not know.

I feel sorry for some Christians who look down on themselves instead of looking up.

How does the devil take away your confidence? By confronting you with unexpected problems.
*"Being confident of this very thing, that he which hath begun a good work in you will perform it until the day of Jesus Christ."*
*Philippians 1:6(KJV)*

*"And this is the confidence that we have in him, that, if we ask anything according to his will, he heareth us: And if we know that he hear us, whatsoever we ask, we know that we have the petitions that we desired of him." I John 5:14-15(KJV)*

But you need to have a relationship with God and know

Him for yourself to have this confidence.

**Why Is the Devil Interested in Our Confidence?**

**I.) Because of our Boldness:** This is a by-product of confidence.

*"The wicked flee when no man pursueth: but the righteous are bold as a lion." Proverbs 28:1(KJV)*

Confidence is a state of mind, but boldness is an action that comes from that state of mind.

In the Book of 1 Samuel 17; David had an encounter with a giant, Goliath. Just the sight of Goliath was enough to intimidate him, but even as a sixteen-year-old boy, he had the boldness to face him.

Every giant problem in your life; business, family, that you are facing has a weakness, and God will open your eyes and expose the weakness of the problem. You will defeat whatever has been proving difficult in your life, in the name of Jesus.

*"There hath no temptation taken you but such as is common to man: but God is faithful, who will not suffer you to be tempted above that ye are able; but will with the temptation also make a way to escape, that ye may be able to bear it." Corinthians 10:13(KJV)*

**ii.) Because of our Ability to Access God:** This occurs through praise and worship. The devil tries to put a stop to this because he desires to hinder our access to God.

**d.) Endeavour to Make Good and Productive Decisions**

The decisions we take in life, lead to the choices we make. What is the meaning of a decision? It is a conclusion or resolution reached after consideration.

In other words, before you decide to do anything, you must have pondered over it, painstakingly observed it, before arriving at your choice.

The choice taken is the grandchild of the decision made. There are good and bad decisions.

**The Concept of Decision Making**

In a bid to make decisions that will yield positive and productive results, you must ask yourself these questions:

**a.) What Do I Want?**

If you are unable to answer this question, you will go nowhere in life. Even when you go for an interview, a time will come when the interviewer will want to know what you want.

What do you want out of life? Do you just want to live life in the name of living without having anything to show for it? What do you desire concerning that job? Is your target only to gain employment in an oil company? Or perhaps you think things just happen?

No! things do not just happen; people make them happen! The fact that I am twenty-two years in marriage means that I know what I want in a marriage. Some did not last for three months in marriage because they did not know what they wanted in marriage.

When you see couples celebrating thirty or fifty years of marriage, you need to realize that someone was willing to pay the price.

Nothing good comes without challenges. It is how you handle it that determines the future repercussions.

## b.) Who Am I?

When God created man, He gave man the ability to be victorious.

*"And God blessed them, and God said unto them, Be fruitful, and multiply, and replenish the earth, and subdue it: and have dominion over the fish of the sea, and over the fowl of the air, and over every living thing that moveth upon the earth."*
*Genesis 1:28(KJV)*

God wants us to be victorious. But today, how people react to challenges, makes me wonder where their victory in Christ lies. They forget who they are and give up easily. They do not know how to press through. There is a miracle with your name written on it, but you need to press through to get it.

Every time you are sick in your body, or your business is in trouble, the devil is asking who you are.

God knows who you are, so also does the devil, but do you know who you are?

The reason why someone who sees himself or herself as a Christian and still submits to other smaller powers to attain success or victory in life, is because they are unaware of who they are.

Whenever the devil attacks you, the forces that are working for you are more than the forces against you. Whenever they tell you at your place of work that you cannot be promoted because you do not have the connection, the forces that are for you, are more than the forces that are against you.

The root of every success whether marital, financial or otherwise, is linked to the decisions you make. The decision you make can either make or mar you.

Decisions based on a foundation of knowledge and sound reasoning would lead to long-term company prosperity, family success, and career success. But conversely, decisions made based on flawed logic, emotion, or incomplete information can quickly put a small or big business out of business.

In the name of Jesus every decision and opportunity that comes your way, you will turn to gold. See something in anything you see around you, never downgrade anything in life.

When the prodigal son journeyed, he spent the money carelessly.

There are some people, the very first week they get their salary, they spend it all. So, I ask, what have you been able to do with what comes into your hands?

If you are a contractor, it is not every time money will come into your hands. There are times money will come and other times when it dries up. But if you do not know how to invest that which has come, and put it into something else that can yield money now and then, so that you can always have liquidity, you will be back on the streets. That is why some people suffer from the begin-again syndrome, today they are rich and the next day they are poor. It is not witchcraft, but stupidity.

If you cannot own your problem, you can never solve it!

In Philippians 4:18; the Bible says; He will supply all our needs according to His riches in heaven. So, if he has supplied all our needs, then evidently, we are supposed to have it.

Whatever it is that has been happening around you or in your family, may the Lord end it today. I release you from the power of every spirit that does not let you take responsibility for your action; I decree and declare that whatever decision has garaged you, limited you or stopped you in life, is reversed.

The prodigal son intended to do business, but instead of doing business, he wasted the money that was allocated to him. He must have thought his father was foolish to have released the funds to him.

The reason why we have companies that have never outlived their founders is because of the children who are wasters. They do not understand what it took their parents to build such a dynasty.

## Examples of Individuals in The Bible Who Made Decisions That Changed the Course of Their Lives

An outstanding and astonishing example of a person who made a good decision and was recognized for it is:

### ● Ruth

The decision Ruth made to follow Naomi introduced her to the lineage of Jesus and gave her name a place in the Bible.(Matthew 1 verses 1-16)

Some made poor decisions that led to them experiencing famine in their lives. They include:

### ● Elimelech

He was a man who made a terrible decision and paid dearly for it. In the Book of Ruth chapter 1 verse 1; Elimelech moved with his wife and children to Moab. After some time, the Bible makes us understand that he died. His decision led to his death. He decided to leave a place of bread, Bethlehem and went to Moab where he met his death.

May your decision not kill you, your children, or end your destiny, in the name of Jesus.

You are a product of decisions. You decided to marry your spouse, no one decided on your behalf. You have made decisions in politics, marriage, in your personal life, and it is these decisions that will produce the outcomes of your life. I decree and declare that every decision you make can only move you to your next level.

- **Abraham**

Another person who made a bad decision was Abraham. The Bible recorded that Abraham had to relocate because there was a famine in the land where he dwelt. So, he decided to leave for Egypt. According to Genesis chapter 12, while he was there, he made a very costly decision where he almost lost his wife because he lied that she was his sister.

Whatever has been happening around you or in your family, may the Lord end it today. I release you from the power of every spirit that does not let you take responsibility for your action. I decree and declare that whatever decision has garaged you, limited you or stopped you in life, is reversed.

FAMINE

## PRAYER

- Father because I am now a child of God, I resist every evil pattern in my family in Jesus' name.
- Circle of economic famine lose your grip over my life in the name of Jesus.

CHAPTER THREE

# SUCCESS NEEDS

Prosperity produces friends but problems reveal their true identities.

CHAPTER TWO

# SUCCESS NEEDS

The word 'need' means to require something because it is essential or very important rather than just desirable. In this context, it means the requirement for success.

You need several things to experience success in life. One of them is the right kind of people.

Esther would not have become a queen without the assistance of Mordecai. If he had not assisted her, she may never have become a queen in a strange land. If someone had not given you a leap in life, it would have been a bit difficult to be at the level that you are right now, because no one succeeds alone. I decree and declare that you will not miss the people you need to succeed in life, in the name of Jesus.

If a leader does not have people to assist him, he will be

stranded in the leadership process. I pray that you will not walk alone, and you will not labour alone. May God fight your battle and give you the right people.

Prosperity produces friends, but problems reveal their true identities. When one is succeeding in life, it is so easy for people to identify with the person. It could be a very tricky period, but my God will deliver you from the wrong set of people in the name of Jesus. It is also important to note that the way we treat people around us, may either spur them to continue rendering help or discourage them from rendering help.

I decree and declare that God will give you the wisdom to deal with people. Every door of opportunity that belongs to you will remain open in the name of Jesus.

People may have forgotten what someone must have said or done to them, but they never forget how they were treated. Whether good or bad, it will remain in their minds for as long as possible.

I will not get into an altercation with anyone because I have grown a thick skin and created every excuse not to be affected by anyone who offends me.

Learn to make people feel welcomed, be warm to them, and be consistent in hospitality –let them know you genuinely care about them. Someone once said: we serve God through people. If you ever find yourself in a position of power, authority, or the place of leadership, always remember that the people under your authority are working for God through you.

## FAVOUR TO SUCCEED

Favour is the bridge that carries a person from failure to success.

It is the power that makes sense out of nonsense; it gives meaning to a meaningless life. God can crown and change the story of a man whom everyone has given up on.

No matter what God gives to you as a blessing, you will enjoy it fully.

Blessings can open doors but it can be shut.
I prophesy that what God is doing for you, will manifest in your life, workplace, marriage in the name of Jesus.

There are a few men God blessed directly, while others inherited their blessing from someone else.
*Genesis 48:22; "Moreover I have given to thee one portion above thy brethren..."*

In the Jewish tradition, only the firstborn gets a double portion, but Joseph the eleventh child got a double portion.

How will a man that is number eleven get a double portion? Because of favour. You may not be the first, but you can be the best because it is God that qualifies the unqualified.
*"And he blessed them that day, saying, In thee shall Israel bless, saying, God make thee as Ephraim and as Manasseh: and he set Ephraim before Manasseh." Genesis 48:20(KJV)*

Why did God make such a powerful pronouncement through Jacob?

Names connect in the spirit realm. What do the names Ephraim and Manasseh mean? Ephraim means fruitfulness, while Manasseh means to forget the past. It also means to be set free from the past.

One of the greatest desires of the devil is to define a person with his or her past, to use it to control his future.
*"Therefore, if any man be in Christ, he is a new creature: old things are passed away; behold, all things are become new."*

*2* Corinthians 5:17

I pronounce a new beginning upon your life and destiny, in Jesus' name.

*"Remember ye not the former things, neither consider the things of old. Behold, I will do a new thing; now it shall spring forth; shall ye not know it? I will even make a way in the wilderness, and rivers in the desert." Isaiah 43:18-19 (KJV)*

Gideon's problem was his past.

*"And the angel of the LORD appeared unto him, and said unto him, The LORD is with thee, thou mighty man of valour." Judges 6:12 (KJV)*

The angel was describing what we could not see; the real Gideon, the hero that was hidden in the zero.

The devil had defined him and garaged him in two ways;

**i.) When the angel made the declaration,** Gideon was being oppressed by the power of his thoughts. In verse 13; he doubted the fact that God was with him. Gideon felt that if God was with him, then he should not be dogged by problems. *Proverbs 23:7; For as he thinketh in his heart, so is he…*

Your thoughts control your words, your words control your actions, which then controls your manifestations.

What has held most people captive is their thoughts.

**ii.) The power of his fathers' house held him down.**

In verse *15… "behold, my family is poor in Manasseh, and I am the least in my father's house".*

2 Corinthians 4:8-9; *"We are troubled on every side, yet not distressed; we are perplexed, but not in despair; persecuted, but not forsaken; cast down, but not destroyed"*

Gideon was being affected by the evil spirits in his father's house, that is why his life was the way it was. The spirits had made themselves comfortable in his life, making Gideon live beneath his rightful standard. All he needed to do, was to change his mindset and break himself loose by proclaiming the spirit of God over his life and be set free from the evil spirits that were dragging him down.

God desires to give you a breakthrough in your job, business, family.

## DROP THE BAGGAGE

A viable need on the path to success is to drop the baggage. Some people slow others down; those who do not have the best intentions concerning the goals of others include:

- Those who lack experience, and despise it in the lives of others.

A lot of people are where they are today because they listened to the wrong people. They did things they ought not to have done because they followed the wrong advice.

When Solomon died, Jeroboam and the children of Israel went to his son and pleaded that he should not make his reign difficult for them, as his father did.

They said in 1Kings12:4: *"Thy father made our yoke grievous: now, therefore, make thou the grievous service of thy father, and his heavy yoke which he put upon us, lighter, and we will serve thee. And he said unto them, Depart yet for three days, then come again to me. And the people parted. And King Rehoboam consulted with the old men, that stood before Solomon his father while he yet lived, and said, how do ye advise that I may answer these people? And they spoke unto him saying if thou wilt be a servant unto this people this day, and wilt serve them, and answer them, and speak good words to them, then they will be thy servants forever."*

But sadly, he listened to the wrong advice. In verse 10, *"And the young men that were grown up with him spake unto him, saying, Thus shalt thou speak unto these people that spake unto thee, saying, Thy father made our yoke heavy, but make thou it lighter unto us; thus shalt thou say unto them, My little finger shall be thicker than my father's loins."*

In verse 12-14; *"So Jeroboam and all the people came to Rehoboam the third day, as the king had appointed, saying, Come to me again the third day. And the king answered the people roughly and forsook the old men's counsel that they gave him; And spake to them after the counsel of the young men, saying, My father made your yoke heavy, and I will add to your yoke: my father also chastised you with whips, but I will chastise you with scorpions." (KJV)*

This young king listened to the wrong people, and that cost him his throne.

The question here is: Who do you listen to? Who is your counselor? On whose instruction do you act? Who is that person in your life that makes you do things you ordinarily would not do? Whose voice do you obey?

It is my prayer that any wrong person positioned in your life; anyone giving you bad counsel to make you do things that are contrary to the will of God for your life, will leave your life in the name of Jesus.

- **Those Without Faith**

It is necessary to be careful about who your personal information is being shared with. If it is shared with the wrong person, there will be a huge price to pay for that.

Many years ago, after my husband had proposed, I was told by the Holy Spirit not to divulge the information to anyone at that time, but although I was tempted to share it, as the news was too good for me to keep to myself, I told no one immediately. A while later, I informed my sister, although I made her promise not to share it with anyone else.

Something profound happened in 2kings7:1: *"Then Elisha said, hear ye the word of the Lord; Thus, saith the LORD, tomorrow about this time shall a measure of fine flour be sold for a shekel, and two measures of barley for a shekel, in the gate of Samaria. Then a lord on whose hand the king leaned answered the man of God and said Behold if the Lord will make windows of heaven, might this thing be? And he said, Behold, thou shalt see it with thine eyes, but shalt not eat thereof"* (KJV).

Some people are naysayers; they never see the possibility in your dreams being achieved. Some even try to dissuade you without any valid reason from pursuing your dreams. If you ever encounter such people, it is wise to separate yourself from them quickly. I decree and declare today that you will escape from that failure in the name of Jesus.

- **Those Envious of You**

The word "envy" means to be desirous of taking what belongs to another, no matter what it may be. Envious people in the society never give the right kind of advice. Their advice does not advance promotion; establishment, increase, or prosperity, instead they keep people low or stagnant in life.

This set of people derive joy in seeing others remain at a certain level in life. So, they downplay the dreams and desires of others, because they fear that others may become more successful than they are in life.

Envious people do not appreciate what they have. They are never satisfied or content with what they have; instead they are ever interested in what belongs to others. They yearn to add what is not theirs to their collection, usually for selfish desires.

When they see families living in serenity and enveloped in love, they become jealous, and wonder why they are not the ones in their shoes. Those were the kind of people who were envious of Isaac, but God made him unstoppable.

I decree and declare that no one will be able to stop you, in the name of Jesus. You are set free from every evil expectation over your family, marriage, and life in the name of Jesus.

## THOSE NEEDED ON THE PATH TO SUCCESS

There are important individuals, needed on the path to success. They are:

- **Those Who Are Where You Desire to Be**

It is important to associate oneself with people who are already where we dream to be someday. This will enable you to know the nitty gritty, the do's and don'ts and the challenges as well as secrets on how to get to that place. For instance, Solomon had elders at his disposal. Though they were elders, they still learned from him. They saw that he carried something great on the inside; something that they felt they did not have enough of, they let down their ego and were willing to learn from him.

- **Those Who Have Your Best Interest at Heart**

It is important to learn and listen to those who genuinely have our best interests at heart. Having such people around, boost a person's morale and drive to continually go after their goals and dreams even when they feel like giving up. They make you believe in yourself even when no one else does. They are a source of strength, and could be the secret ingredient for some goal getters and pace setters.

- **Those with Positive Energy**

In the society, those who have negative energy, tend to drown those that surround them. They never proffer any form of help. So, it is advisable to converse and build relationships only with people who are filled with positive energy, as they will help to improve one's life to success extraordinaire.

- **Those that Plant Seeds of Encouragement When Things are Bad**

These set of people act as pillars of support when things are hard and uncertain. They are always available to lend a helping hand, give a listening ear, or give an advice or a solution that will help that person believe in his or herself again. Associating with these kind of people can make an unimaginable dream become a reality.

- **Life Coaches/ Motivational Speakers**

There are experienced people with skills who empower those who lack these skills with secrets that could make them better in life. They are known for being open books. They do not sugar coat things. Such people challenge those around them to be better. This trait makes them one of the most important types of people to have in life.

- **Loyal People**

These are another breed of genuine people to have on the path to success. In the book of Mark Chapter 2, we see the story of the paralysed man, who was brought in through the roof, with the help of his friends, for him to be healed. They did not give up because there was a crowd around Jesus. They were not deterred by how impossible the situation looked because they were willing to help their friend.

This is the mindset we must have when relating to other people. Never give up on helping others. Remember that we are blessed because we have been blessed.

- **Inspirational Figures**

These are people who are admired in the society. They are people who have followed the path we intend to follow or are already following such paths. Most times, they are widely read about and studied by those who admire their success stories.
It is important to respect their persons no matter what and focus on the primary goal which is to learn their ways.

- **God**

We cannot do without God in the journey to success in life. It is paramount to always listen, follow, and adhere to all instructions from God on the path to success.
You must also make strong personal decisions that will guide you on this route. You must:

- **Decide to be a champion/victor**

If you make this decision, then the power of God will defeat every one of your oppositions. Some people end up on the seat of self-pity and hopelessness because they have been discouraged by what fellow humans told them about themselves. While others get there, because of disappointments from close friends and family.

- **See yourself as a champion/winner.**

When you look at yourself, what do you see? If you look at yourself and see a loser, then that is what you are and there is nothing that God can do, but if you see yourself as a victor, then there is nothing the devil can do about it.

*"And there we saw the giants, the sons of Anak, which come of the giants: and we were in our sight as grasshoppers, and so we were in their sight." Numbers 13:33(KJV)*

This was the assessment of ten out of the twelve spies that went to spy out the land. They identified themselves as grasshoppers. and they died in the wilderness as such.

Our culture has programmed us to believe that when we get to a certain age, we become dependents. We begin to look for who to fall back on, who to spoon-feed us. You have to deprogram and free yourself from that set mentality.
Gideon had thirty -two thousand men who looked like champions but they were not.

- **Impose what you know on what you are thinking**

In Genesis 17:17; when God told Abraham that his wife will have a child, he laughed. In chapter18:12, Sarah laughed, they did so because of what they were seeing. They saw that what was on the ground, did not agree with what God was saying.

*"Is anything too hard for the LORD? At the time appointed I will return unto thee, according to the time of life, and Sarah shall have a son." Genesis 18:14(KJV)*

It was their situation that made them forget that there is nothing too hard for God.

One of the reasons we do not get what we are looking for is because our minds are loaded with unbelief, as a result of the physical reports confronting us.

Deny every iota of unbelief concerning that situation in your life right now.

You need to deny it, close that chapter, and move on.

## PRAYER

- From today, I declare that I connect with the right people that will spur me on positively in my journey to success in the name of Jesus.
- I pray that God will give you the wisdom to deal with people. Every door of opportunity that belongs to you will remain open in the name of Jesus.
- I pronounce a new beginning upon your life and destiny, in Jesus' name.

CHAPTER FOUR

# STRATEGIES TO SUCCEED

> God's word
> will never produce
> a difference or work in
> your life until
> you believe.

CHAPTER FOUR

# STRATEGIES TO SUCCEED

A strategy is a plan of action designed to achieve a goal or aim. It is something created, to ensure that success is sure. The plan made for the previous year might have fulfilled its purpose and brought great success, but it does not mean that it would work in the following year. It is time to draw up another strategic plan for that business, marriage, education, career. A strategy must be implemented to help determine how to win in the seasons ahead.

What does it mean to succeed? To succeed is to excel at every given opportunity in life. It means to stand out amongst others; to record achievements where others have not, to have something to show for a living. You cannot succeed without having a strategic plan!

A man who goes to battle knows that adequate preparation is necessary if he plans to win the battle.

If one chooses to succeed in life or desires to be distinguished by God, then the decision to fully trust in Him must be made and that is where faith comes in.

God's word will never produce a difference or work in your life until you believe.

Many people go to church, hear the word of God, and do not believe it. And so, the word does not work in their lives. They are hardened, so the word does not affect their lives.

Fornicators are still fornicating, those cheating in business, continue to do so, gossipers still gossip, because they refuse to accept His word.

The word "believe" means to accept trustfully. You believe to be saved, delivered, set free, because the word covers everything.

*"For verily I say unto you, That whosoever shall say unto this mountain, Be thou removed, and be thou cast into the sea; and shall not doubt in his heart, but shall believe that those things which he saith shall come to pass; he shall have whatsoever he saith. Therefore, I say unto you, what things soever ye desire, when ye pray, believe that ye receive them, and ye shall have them."*
Mark 11:23-24(KJV)

*"And Jesus answering saith unto them, Have faith in God"*
Mark 11:22 (KJV).

Faith means to trust and believe something or someone or to blindly follow an instruction. It is difficult to take commands from someone whose judgement is not trusted, or from someone you lack faith in. The Bible dwells a lot on the need to have faith in God.

*"But without faith, it is impossible to please him: for he that cometh to God must believe that he is and that he is a rewarder of them that diligently seek him."*
*Hebrews 11:6(KJV)*

From the scripture above, the word diligently could mean that the task may take a very long time, but because you believe, you will steadfastly continue to do it, because you know you will eventually get it done.

May your faith work for you in every area of your life as you journey through the earth in the name of Jesus.

*"My people are destroyed for lack of knowledge: because thou hast rejected knowledge, I will also reject thee, that thou shalt be no priest to me: seeing thou hast forgotten the law of thy God, I will also forget thy children." Hosea 4:6(KJV)*

## FAITH TO SUCCEED
### Why do we need faith?

*"And what shall I more say? For the time would fail me to tell of Gedeon, and of Barak, and Samson, and Jephthae; of David also, and Samuel, and of the prophets: who through faith subdued kingdoms] wrought righteousness, obtained promises, stopped the mouths of lions." Hebrews 11:32-33(KJV)*

The devil destroys people because they lack the knowledge and the basics of God. That is why he can attack people's finances and succeed, because they do not understand their relationship with God, in terms of money, and other areas of their lives.

You need faith to believe in God and live the Christian life.

Faith is substance, it is evidence. Evidence can be seen, but not faith; what makes faith evident is the word of God.

In other words, faith is believing that you are what the Bible says you are. It is believing that you can do what the Bible says you can do. The Bible says; *"I can do all things through Christ which strengthens me."* Phillipians 4:13 (KJV) It is taking the Bible and making it work for you.

**How Can we have Faith?**

Praying without faith is a waste of time; do not pray to have faith. Fasting does not give you faith either, it only puts you in the right mood to use your faith.

*"So, then faith cometh by hearing, and hearing by the word of God."* Romans 10:17(KJV)

*"This book of the law shall not depart out of thy mouth; but thou shalt meditate therein day and night, that thou mayest observe to do according to all that is written therein: for then thou shalt make thy way prosperous, and then thou shalt have good success."*
*Joshua 1:8(KJV)*

From the book of Romans chapter 10, faith comes by hearing, meaning that it is a continuous process.
Joshua won his battles because he meditated on the word. When the word of God enters you, by the time it is needed, it will rise and work for you.

There are four sets of people mentioned in Matthew 13:18-58.

- Those who hear the word, but as soon as they hear, the devil comes and snatches what they have heard.

- Those who hear, welcome the word, and receive the word; but do not have depth, so, the word does not get to the heart.

For these category of people, when trouble comes, it will sweep them off their feet and they will fall. If they promote everyone in their office and exclude them, they may decide to stop going to church.

- Those that have received the word, but are sown on thorns; they are entangled with the deceitfulness of riches and the cares of this world.

  Be hardworking but look for a balance. Do not neglect God in the chase of business, money, and the things of this life.

- Those that are planted on good ground. The proof that your life is a good ground is that your life must bring forth fruit, that means there must be a sign.

  Good grounds are for those who hear the word, comprehend it and it dwells in their heart genuinely. *"Colossians 3:16; Let the word of Christ dwell in you richly in all wisdom…"*

**Other strategies are:**
- Conquering your circumstances by conquering your thoughts.

One of the worst things you can do to yourself is to underestimate the power and the influence of your thoughts. The ability to think is one of the most essential abilities given to man by God. He expects us to think. It is an unexplainable ability.

Your thoughts can either help to build the foundation for success, or it can also build the foundation for failure.
*Proverbs 23:7; "For as he thinketh in his heart, so is he…"*

The word thinketh means 'a gatekeeper'. Whosoever controls your thoughts will eventually control your spirit.

*"Then when lust hath conceived, it bringeth forth sin: and sin, when it is finished, bringeth forth death."* James 1:15(KJV)

Lord help me, cleanse my thoughts with the blood of Jesus.

The fear of failure and the fear of defeat, when conceived will produce failure and defeat. The fear that you have that you will never succeed in life, or that you are a write-off, or that nothing good will ever come out of your life will produce failure. The faith for success when conceived will produce success.

Some Christians blame others when things do not work out the way they planned and forget to blame themselves. In their minds, they cannot see anything big or great; whatever they see is small. Their thoughts are what destroys them.

Whenever you make a promise, realize that there is a giant that will try to stop you.

David was able to defeat Goliath because, in his thoughts, nothing could stop him.

There are some of you, your trouble may seem so big, the situation may seem unsolvable, but the God we serve is more than able to provide a solution to all the problems.

*"Casting down imaginations, and every high thing that exalteth itself against the knowledge of God, and bringing into captivity every thought to the obedience of Christ."* *2 Corinthians 10:5(KJV)*

Some Christians go to church, they pray and do the needful, but do not believe they can overcome what they are going through.

You must believe that whatever you are going through, you can begin to defeat it from this moment.

- **By defeating the devil in the mind**

*"There hath no temptation taken you but such as is common to man: but God is faithful, who will not suffer you to be tempted above that ye are able; but will with the temptation also make a way to escape, that ye may be able to bear it."*
1 Corinthians 10:13(KJV)

When God speaks to you, He does so through your spirit, but when the devil speaks to you, he does so through your mind.

The battleground between you and the devil is your mind! *"And be not conformed to this world: but be ye transformed by the renewing of your mind, that ye may prove what is that good, and acceptable, and perfect, will of God."*
Romans 12:2(KJV)

*"In whom the god of this world hath blinded the minds of them which believe not, lest the light of the glorious gospel of Christ, who is the image of God, should shine unto them."*
Corinthians 4:4(KJV)

From the scriptures, Paul warns us not to allow the devil to dominate our minds because he is the god of this world. He rules the world but not you and me.

The devil works on the mind!

1 Corinthians 10:13; explains this concept very well. It dissects it into 4 parts:

- *"There hath no temptation taken you but such as is common to man"*

If the devil can defeat you in your mind, he can defeat you in your life. One of the first things the devil does in times of tribulation is that he makes you feel like you have the biggest problem in life. And he will knock you out with it if you do not believe in God.

*"The thing that hath been, it is that which shall be; and that which is done is that which shall be done: and there is no new thing under the sun. Is there anything whereof it may be said, See, this is new? It hath been already of old time, which was before us. There is no remembrance of former things; neither shall there be any remembrance of things that are to come with those that shall come after." Ecclesiastes 1:9-11(KJV)*

From the scripture above, the Bible clearly shows that whatever problem is confronting us is not new. Your story can be the same.

My husband told me a story, about a man who was very poor and fed up with life. He had a little amount of food left, and he told himself, he would eat it and kill himself. He believed that no one loved or cared for him. So, he climbed a tree, tied a rope to it and sat down to eat. When he was done eating the rice, he threw the leaf away, and then a naked passer-by saw it, picked it up, thanked God, and licked off the food remnant on the leaf. After observing the scene, he said to himself, if this man given his dire condition would not take his life, why should I? And so, he did not go through with the suicide.

- *"But God is faithful"*

The word faithful means reliable, dependable, trustworthy. God gave Joseph a dream that he will be a great man. But not too long after he received the dream; he went to meet his brothers who plotted and threw him into a pit. Instead of coming up, he was going down.

Joseph kept going down, he descended from a slave to a 'senior slave'. Then to a prisoner from where things began to change.

God's plans are different from ours; He is God alone and He makes things happen the way He wants.

*"Know therefore that the LORD thy God, he is God, the faithful God, which keepeth covenant and mercy with them that love him and keep his commandments to a thousand generations" Deutoronomy 7:9(KJV)*

*"And I saw heaven opened, and behold a white horse, and he that sat upon him was called Faithful and True, and in righteousness, he doth judge and makes war." Revelation 19:11(KJV)*

*"But the Lord is faithful, who shall establish you, and keep you from evil." 2 Thessalonians 3:3(KJV)*

- *"who will not suffer you to be tempted above that ye are able"*

Do you know that you can overcome whatever you are going through?

If you are a child of God, whatever pressure or tension is around you, the spirit of God will raise a standard against the devil.

*"But he said unto her, Thou speakest as one of the foolish women speaketh. What? Shall we receive good at the hand of God, and shall we not receive evil? In all this did not Job sin with his lips." Job 2:10(KJV)*

Job lost his property, children, and health, but his faith in God never wavered.

- *"but will with the temptation also make a way to escape, that ye may be able to bear it"*

With every challenge, trial, trouble, and tribulation, there is a way of escape. God has already made a way, what is needed is to find the way and step into it.

In your workplace, some people desire to hold you down and some cannot sleep at night because of you; but in all, God makes a way that no man can block.

- **By Arising and Building**

The word 'arise' means to get up, to stand.

Naturally, if God is saying 'arise' he is asking you to get up and do something; concerning your life, business, job, etc.
You will arise and achieve success; you will arise and be promoted, you will arise for an increase, you will arise for expansion, you will arise and build goodly houses.
In a bid to do so, there are things to take into consideration:

- **You need to feel discomfort to achieve success**

When you feel comfortable with your present state, you will never get up to do anything. The only thing that makes a man go for success is when he believes he can do better.

What can make you strive for something better in life? It is when you feel within you that what you have is not enough.

The difference between those who are comfortable with where they are and those who are not is the hunger within them to do better.

Your ability to arise is in you, God has already decided that you will arise, and the only way to do this is to aspire to do something better.

The Bible said, according to Nehemiah, by the reason of the good hand of the Lord upon his head, the king granted him that which he wanted.

After Nehemiah went back to Jerusalem, he said; let us arise and build.

### What Do You Need to Build?

To obtain all-round success in all areas of a person's life, there is an immense need to work on the following;

- **Your career/profession**

Whatever little business you are doing, whatever its worth, try to aspire to double its worth. Save, put the money aside, and grow the business.

At the time in my life when I was growing my business, my business was very rich while I was poor. I was paying myself.

There were times, I would get my salary and give it to those who were in need. I would then exhaust my salary, and start feeding mainly on cassava flakes, even though I had millions in my business account. I would behave myself wisely and manage myself through the month. As a result, many years later, I could now afford several of the things I needed.

You get to a stage in life where you lose count of what you have because you disciplined yourself at the beginning of your growth.

- **Your children**

It is the quality of time and effort you put into the lives of your children that will qualify them for a better tomorrow.

- **Your home**

*Proverbs 14:1; "Every wise woman buildeth her house: but the foolish plucketh it down with her hands."*

Build your home with patience, understanding, prayers, and never take anything for granted. As you build your home, you are building yourself. Be a bit creative, being creative does not need to be expensive.

- **Your Church**

Nothing guarantees an individual's success than giving one's services whenever needed. Be willing to do God's work at convenient and inconvenient times, winning more souls and genuinely enjoying the time spent in God's presence.

## KING JEHOSHAPHAT'S SUCCESS STRATEGY

*"It came to pass after this also, that the children of Moab, and the children of Ammon, and with them, others beside the Ammonites, came against Jehoshaphat to battle", verse 4; "And Judah gathered themselves together, to ask the help of the LORD: even out of all the cities of Judah they came to seek the LORD"*
*2Chronicles 20:1 (KJV).*

**The help Jehoshaphat was asking for in the above scripture was the strategy needed to win the battle.** Many times, when people are faced with situations, they ask God to take them out of it, but God says no! The only way to take you out is to give you a strategy on how to get out of the situation.

The plan mapped out for what we require to tackle now, might be obsolete for tomorrow. In other words, the plan needed to succeed in one location may be different from the plan needed to succeed in another location.

Strategic plans need to be altered to suit the time, location, and the parties involved. *In verse 15; "And he said, hearken ye, all Judah, and ye inhabitants of Jerusalem, and thou king*

*Jehoshaphat, thus saith the LORD unto you, be not afraid nor dismayed because of this great multitude; for the battle is not yours, but God's" (KJV).*

Whatever situation or challenges we are faced with in life is not a battle for us but of the Lord. When our father in heaven is consulted because of the battles we are confronted with in life, we will surely be victorious at the end of it all. God says, ask me and you will get it. He will give you a strategy that will make all issues become history.

*In verse 20-21; "And they arose early in the morning and went forth into the wilderness of Tekoa: and as they went forth, Jehoshaphat stood and said, Hear me, O Judah, and ye inhabitants of Jerusalem; Believe in the LORD your God, so shall ye be established; believe his prophets, so shall ye prosper. And when he had consulted with the people, he appointed singers unto the LORD, and that should praise the beauty of holiness, as they went out before the army, and to say, Praise the LORD; for his mercy endureth forever." (KJV)*

Jehoshaphat called on God Almighty for a strategy and God came to his rescue by providing him with one. and Jehoshaphat stepped out and actualized the strategy that God gave to him.

When God provides a strategy, it is mandatory to work with it, no matter how weird it may seem at the time. The Bible makes us understand that His mercies endureth forever. The strategy needed to become parents, to buy a house or a car, to maintain good health, God will give to you, as He gave it to Jehoshaphat.

In verse 22 the Bible says; *"And when they began to sing and to praise, the LORD set ambushments against the children of*

*Ammon, Moab, and mount Seir, which were come against Judah; and they were smitten" (KJV)*

As Jehoshaphat and the children of Israel began to implement the strategy, He laid an ambush against their enemies.

When you work on the strategic plan that God has given to you, you will win. The people of the house of Judah were excited because they did not have to lift a finger, but they worked on their God given strategy. Sometimes, all you need is a word. When you have a strategy and you make it work, you will become a mother, a father, a business tycoon, a house owner, in the name of Jesus.

God gave me a strategy that paved the way for me to meet my husband many years back. Before I got married, I asked God to give me a husband. Two to three people showed up at a time. They were all influential. One came to my office with a briefcase full of dollars to induce me into marrying him. Another boastfully requested that I give him my account number so he can send money to me. But after I prayed, God told me neither of them was the man for me. I took time off work to pray because I wanted God to show me what to do concerning the issue of my meeting the right suitors for my life. God told me to send away the people that were in my house at that time and clean up the house. I thought about it. It seemed like quite a hard task to do, so I resisted it and kept on praying. But then, God did not speak again. Then it hit me that I had to go with the strategy that He had given to me. So, I summoned up courage, got an apartment for those living with me, and moved them out of my home as He had instructed.

Two months later, a friend called me and told me about a

spiritual father who was in town. She told me he would pray for us, so I accepted because I love to pray and to be prayed for. I left early for the office that day and left a word with my manager to call me when they showed up. I had to go out to fix some problems I was having with my laptop. My manager forgot to call me when they turned up. When I arrived home, my friend called to find out what had happened which I explained to her. She agreed to come over and pick me up to go and visit the man of God. When we got there, we were asked to wait for him at the lounge. By the time he came out to see us, we all stood up to acknowledge his presence. It was uncomfortable for me to do so because while growing up, I had been trained that when a man steps into a place; the lady if seated, remains seated even while exchanging pleasantries. So, I was a bit surprised when I found myself on my feet. I did not know what had come over me, but there was something about him that made me do that unknowingly.

After exchanging pleasantries, we sat down, and then they started asking him questions, I wondered if they had forgotten the primary reason for the visit, so I quickly drew his attention to the reason why we were there for prayers! He smiled and said he had not forgotten. When he began to pray for us, I suddenly saw myself being lifted and positioned by his side, and then the Lord said: "this is your husband". It was a difficult instruction to follow at first, because I never imagined being married to a pastor. But I knew that I had to follow God's plan for my life, and I am grateful I did.

I prophesy into your life, that the strategy you need to succeed in marriage, business, career, God will give to you.

## STEPS TO IMPLEMENT STRATEGIC PLANS

- **Seek the Face of God**

*"Ask, and it shall be given you; seek, and ye shall find; knock, and it shall be opened unto you."*
*Matthew 7:7 (KJV)*

Be willing to ask God for directions, or the right way to follow to implement that plan. Ask him for the best route no matter how strange it may seem, to achieving and seeing that plan come to life. It is because people lack this understanding that they start businesses for which they lack the essential knowledge, skills, and passion. Endeavour to follow God's unique plan for your own success.

From inception, God mapped out unique success strategies for every one of us. May God open doors of opportunities for you. May He teach your hands how to maximize opportunities as they come, and may you be able to use them to your advantage in the name of Jesus.

- **Identify Where You Are**

Where are you right now? On what level, are you? You need to be honest with yourself. In business terms, this is referred to as **S.W.O.T analysis;**

**"S"** stands for **Strength:**

Strength distinguishes one person from another. So, it is necessary to tap into it when the need arises. The challenge that we have in this world is that we abandon our strengths and try to copy someone else forgetting we are not them.

**"W"** represents **Weaknesses:**

We need to be honest with ourselves to identify the areas of our weaknesses. When I interview people, I always ask them about their areas of weaknesses. Many claim to have none, but it is an error because as humans, we all have weaknesses. It is good to acknowledge the fact that you have weaknesses, so you can tackle them head-on or begin to work squarely on them.

If that step is not taken, the devil will capitalize on it and use it to his advantage. Some people cannot handle leadership positions, while some cannot handle success. It ruins them instead of making them. The only way forward is to first acknowledge the fact that there is a problem, then work on it.

**"O" represents Opportunities:**

It is important to recognize all opportunities that come your way.

**"T" stands for Threats:**

The administrative policies of a nation can become a threat to people in the society and can endanger their businesses. The environment can also be a threat, so also the competitors around. We must try to understand the environment we find ourselves before venturing into anything.

- **Determine Where You Are Going**

After a proper re-evaluation has been done of the position and level one is in life, then the next step is to determine where to go from there in order to move forward.

In the book of Genesis Chapter 41, the Bible made us understand that after Joseph interpreted the dream of Pharaoh, he was appointed into authority. Remember that while he was giving the interpretation, God gave him a strategic plan.

He told him to expect plenty in the land in the first seven years, but that the following seven years would be years of famine.

To ensure that the famine season will not affect the everyday routine in their businesses and their economic situation at that time, He told him to tell them to use the bountiful seven years to gather and prepare for the rainy days ahead.

*In verse 49, "And Joseph gathered corn as the sand of the sea, very much, until he left numbering; for it was without number. Verse 52; "And the name of the second called he Ephraim: For God hath caused me to be fruitful in the land of my affliction" (KJV).*

Why did God bless him in the land of affliction? Because he had a strategy that propelled him to be fruitful, and he used it. In times of famine, a strategy is needed to survive and win. It will be very outrageous to remain indolent and be expectant during this period. The Bible tells us that when others were experiencing famine, the land of Egypt was spared. There was enough bread in the land for the people, because they listened to the words spoken by the servant of God.

## PRAYER

- Father, I receive the right strategy to succeed in every aspect of my life, in Jesus' name.

CHAPTER FIVE

# THE PATH TO SUCCESS

> Never compare someone else's success to yours

CHAPTER FIVE

# THE PATH TO SUCCEED

The road to achieving goals, strategies, and purposes in life, is never smooth. There are challenges and obstacles along the way but the determination to remain focused on the goal is what guarantees success. To determine the path to success, you must:

**1.) Locate Your Assignment**
Never compare someone else's success to yours. This is one of the reasons why people get frustrated in life. Every human being on earth is born to succeed. There are ingredients we all carry that open the gate to our success. Locate what that occupation or trade is and strive to accomplish it. For example, I know my place of assignment here on earth, and as I continue to function, success is bound to always occur.

## 2.) Acquire skill, training, and expertise

Show me a successful man, and you will see a man who is skilled in his trade or very proficient in his enterprise. In other words, the level of success attained is determined by our level of awareness, understanding, and knowledge of a certain field.

The point to emphasize here is that no matter what a man does for a living, he should get himself properly trained before he fully ventures into that enterprise.

It is my wish for everyone to prosper, but your prosperity does not only depend on my wish, but it also depends on the development of your mind(3 John 2). We all need to improve our level of skill and efficiency in our area of enterprise. It is necessary to acquire professional help from those who are already skilled so we can be better and do the things we do better.

Show me a successful man, and I will show you a man who made use of the opportunities that came his way.

In the society we find ourselves today, people imitate others. This is wrong! I will never imitate anyone because I am not them, and vice versa. The reason why there is bitterness, envy, animosity, competition, rivalry in the church is that people think that some other person's place or position is better than theirs. So, they bicker and try to pull down their fellow Christian brother and sister because they have difficulty accepting what God has put on the inside of them. A life spent that way is unhealthy and leads to unfulfilled accomplishment.

## 3.) Prepare to Work Hard

*"What does it profit, my brethren, though a man say he hath faith, and have not worked? can faith save him?*

*James 2:14 (KJV)*

After fasting and praying, the only way God can step in is for you to mix your faith with work. Work means action, do something! It is after you work that God Almighty will begin to add favour to your work.

*"If a brother or sister be naked and destitute of daily food, and one of you say unto them, Depart in peace, be ye warmed and filled; notwithstanding ye give them those things which are needful to the body; what doth it profit?" James 2:15-16(KJV).*

If we rely only on faith without backing it with works, there will be nothing for God to bless. He only blesses 'something.' Bring out what is on the inside to experience extraordinary success.

## 4.) Prepare Ahead for the goals.

Success is meant for thinkers, it is not innate, it can be learnt. It is said that ideas rule the world. But these ideas do not come through shallow minds, they resonate from the reservoir of our capacity to think.

The fact that a major task was accomplished in any department of life, is not the end of the road. We live in a very dynamic environment, one in which the indices of an individual's success is determined by his ability to be able to come up with a plan.

If someone puts ten million naira in your hands; without any concrete plans designated for it, it will be squandered in no time. It is not only about the amount of money in your account, but it is also about your capability to sit and think through on how the money will be spent strategically.

For married couples to enjoy more blissful years in

marriage, they can draft out a plan on how to make their marriage more beautiful as the years go by.

Never capitalize on making money alone, instead go after rendering of services as well. Some people get into business and all they are interested in is when the money will start rolling in. This is a limited way of thinking. When people are in need, they look out for those who can render the services required. It is best to make the business as reachable as possible to people. It should be flexible. Make the environment of the business-friendly and accommodating, and more people will endeavour to patronize the business.

## 5.) Do not Waste Opportunities that Come Around

*"The slothful man roasteth not that which he took in hunting, but the substance of a diligent man is precious"* Proverbs 12:27 *(KJV)*.

A slothful man is a lazy man; a diligent man is a man who does not waste opportunities. Seize the moment!

Look for that opportunity, utilize it, and your success will be guaranteed.

A person's success is not dependent on another, it is only dependent on that person and God. And if opportunities are not recognized in due time, they could be taken by someone else who is ready to utilize the opportunity.

*"I returned and saw under the sun, that the race is not for the swift, nor the battle to the strong, neither yet bread to the wise, nor yet riches to men of understanding, nor yet favour to men of skill; but time and chance happeneth to them all"* Ecclesiastes 9:11 *(KJV)*.

## 6.) Put God First

God promised that if we put Him before anyone or

anything else, then our needs can be accomplished.

*"For the LORD God is a sun and shield: the LORD will give grace and glory: no good thing will he withhold from them that walk uprightly" Psalm 84:11 (KJV).*

### 7.) Deal with Enemies Through Prayers

For you to be a success in life, you must be able to deal with the enemy. The reason why Africa has a large number of occult operators is because many people cannot discover their real selves and work at it to produce success for themselves. So, when they see someone else succeeding, they strive to pull them down.

*"And a man's foes shall be they of his household" Matthew 10:36 (KJV).*

## How Do You Locate Opportunities?
### 1.) Through Discernment

There is a difference between perception and discernment. Perception speaks of the five senses. But there are tendencies for what is perceived to get distorted due to our thoughts, making us perceive wrongly.

What you perceive is controlled by your upbringing. The way I see things is different from the way you see things. I can see a glass of water, as half full, and another person can see that same glass as half empty.

Both of us may be right but the difference in our perception is that I am optimistic, while the other person is pessimistic.

Most times your perception can create a form of deception for you. That is why sometimes people see things wrongly. They look at someone and judge them based on their outward appearance.

In the Bible, Samuel was guilty of this. God told Him to go and appoint a king for Him in the house of Jesse. Samuel, a seasoned prophet, got there and decided to operate with his physical five senses. He wanted to go for someone who had the physique of a king, but God had to redirect his thinking and perception.

This scenario also played out in the case of Lot and Abraham. When Abraham asked Lot to choose the land he desired to go into, He chose based on only his five senses. He did not know it was going to be a place of distress.

Many of you have been following Sodom and Gomorrah, and then you wonder what is happening. It is because you are not led. You are using your five senses instead of consulting the Spirit of the living God. When you consult the Holy Spirit, it resonates in your discernment.

*"The manifestation of the Spirit is given to every man to profit withal."*

*1 Corinthians 12:7 (KJV)*

*"To another the working of miracles; to another prophecy; to another discerning of spirits; to another divers kind of tongues; to another the interpretation of tongues."*

*1 Corinthians 12:10 (KJV)*

*"But strong meat belongeth to them that are of full age, even those who by reason of use have their sense exercised to discern both good and evil."*

*Hebrews 5:14 (KJV)*

Discernment is associated with operating in the Spirit.

## How Do You Operate in Discernment?

- By Receiving The Holy Spirit

  After receiving the Holy Spirit, the Spirit of discernment is released.

## The Holy Spirit has a big part to play when gunning for success. We need the Holy Spirit because:

### * He Will Show Us Things to Come

*"I have yet many things to say unto you, but ye cannot bear them now. Howbeit when he, the Spirit of truth, is come, he will guide you into all truth: for he shall not speak of himself; but whatsoever he shall hear, that shall he speak: and he shall shew you things to come..."*
John 16:12-15 (KJV).

When the Lord says the Holy Spirit will show us things to come; He is not telling us to visit false prophets or soothsayers or build fake temples for false prophets. Instead, He is declaring that we need to be in connection with the Holy Spirit, and understand Him better for us to be in tune with Him.

When we do, He will open our eyes to show us how impossibilities can become possible. If there is anything that has blinded your eyes, causing you not to see a solution to that situation, I decree and declare that the Holy Spirit will minister to you, He will begin to show you what to do.

- ### He will Instill His Power Within

*"But ye shall receive power, after that, the Holy Ghost comes upon you: and ye shall be witnesses unto me both in Jerusalem and in all Judea, and Samaria, and unto the uttermost part of the earth"*

*Acts 1:8(KJV)*

It means before the door can be opened the power of the Holy Ghost must dwell in your life, he must take over your being, your life and destiny, your children as well.

- **By Renewing Your Mind to God's word**

*"And be not conformed to this world; but be transformed by the renewing of your mind, that ye may prove what is that good and acceptable, and perfect will of God."*
Romans 12:2(KJV)

The act of not doing something regularly will hinder the possibility of attaining perfection in that thing. Perception is transformed into discernment, by the act of continuously listening and studying the word of God.

There are times you will get it wrong because your spirit will yield to the flesh. Do not be discouraged, continue to exercise your faith.

I decree and declare that from now on, the Holy Spirit will lead you.

## 2.) Create Ideas to Meet the Needs of Others

A businessman must be eager to meet needs every day. People who only think about what they will get, never get anything. Only those who set out looking for needs to meet, make it in life.

*"For I was hungry and ye gave me meat: I was thirsty and ye gave me drink: I was a stranger, and ye took me in"*
*Matthew 25:35(KJV)*

By finding a need and meeting the need, you create an

opportunity for your own needs to be met. May you locate your opportunity.

**3.) Choose Your Location Wisely**

There is a need to ask the question; Where will the business or company succeed? Will they need the product or service there?

I prophesy to you that as you find your place, it will be a blessing to you. People are thinking of moving out of the country; others thinking of leaving town, unaware that God has set men up to create opportunities. As you work in the house of God and meet the needs of others; your own needs will be met, in Jesus' name.

## SUCCEEDING THROUGH OPPORTUNITIES

The word 'opportunity' is an event created by God to bring advancement and progress to someone's life.

Why is it that anytime there is an important appointment to keep something deliberately holds you back?

When a man misses his opportunities; it could be because he is ignorant, blind, or being manipulated by a dark force.

I prophesy into your life; you will locate your place of opportunity, you will meet a need, that will transform into the beginning of your success story.

In 1 Chronicles 12:32; the Bible shows us two powerful things about the children of Issachar. Issachar was the fifth son of his father. The number 'five' stands for grace.

**The Bible says:**

1.) The children of Issachar understood the times.

When a man understands the times, it means he can recognize

opportunities when they come.

2.) They were made head.

When a man or woman knows what to do with opportunities, he will always be the head and not the tail. He will be on top and never beneath, and will never be dominated.

Immaturity will blind you from opportunities.

When opportunities come your way, some forces try to divert it.

When God opens up a need in the church, it is because He wants to give someone an opportunity to change position in life.

Wherever you find yourself in life, there is an opportunity.

The word 'opportunity' is an event created by God to bring advancement and progress to someone's life.

I see an opportunity for advancement and promotion; it will not pass you by, in the name of Jesus.

## PRAYER

- Lord! grant me the ability to know what to do with opportunities
- Lord grant me the ability to recognize an opportunity, and utilize it.

CHAPTER SIX

# SUCCESS IN BUSINESS

> The richest people in the world today were those who succeeded in meeting the needs of people

CHAPTER SIX

# SUCCESS IN BUSINESS

A business is someone's regular occupation, profession, or trade that deals solely with a specific line of work. It also has to do with our ability to meet the needs around us.

Business is people!

The richest people in the world today were those who succeeded in meeting the needs of people. It is all about meeting needs. Many people worry about making money, ignoring their customers in the process. The man who started the business of making flip flops has became very rich because he met affordable needs.

In the Book of Luke Chapter 5, there came a time, God

had a need. He desired to preach to the people around Him. A man named Simon Peter met the need by giving God access to his boat. In return, God blessed his business.

If we must succeed in business, we must allow God to use our boat.

May you not do business alone; may you do business with God in the name of Jesus.

When you do business with God you can only make profit, you cannot lose. Whatever it is that you do, you will experience success in the name of Jesus.

How do you think a small-scale industry or a micro-business can enter a market?

It is better for a bungalow to crash than a skyscraper. In other words, it is better to start small and lose small money, than to start big and lose big.

You learn better in business when you start small.

In the Book of 1 Kings 17, there is the story of Prophet Elijah and the widow of Zarephath that also shows the benefit of doing business with God.

*"And the word of the Lord came unto him, saying, Arise, get thee to Zarephath, which belongeth to Zidon, and dwell there: behold, I have commanded a widow there to sustain thee",*
*1 kings 17:8(KJV)*
*"And as she was going to fetch it, he called to her, and said, Bring me, I pray thee, a morsel of bread in thine hand"*
*1kings 17:1(KJV)*

At first, the woman did not respond in line with what God had told Elijah. Instead, she told him that she did not have food to give to him as it was a period of famine.

Elijah told the widow to prepare the little food she had for him and her household and prophesied, that the barrel of meal, the last bit of food she had in her house, would not run dry. So, she did as Elijah instructed. As a result, she had enough food for herself and the prophet Elijah throughout the time of the famine. The food kept multiplying because she obeyed God.

I decree and declare that as we allow God to take first place in everything that pertains to us; the barrel of meal in our hands will not be depleted.

Whatever we do will amount to success. We will not fail, in the name of Jesus.

When God was done using the boat of Peter, He gave him surplus. Stingy people cannot enjoy surplus. Because they hold on to what they have too closely.

While some are stingy to those around them, others are stingy to themselves, and even to God.

Jesus told Simon Peter to go a little bit forward into the deep and throw in the net to catch the fish. God showed him the direction in which he would be successful because he allowed God to use his boat.

In verse 4, Jesus asked him to launch out into the deep. He wanted him to do something different. To succeed yearly, do things differently.

When five to ten people are doing the same thing, and one of them decides to step out and introduce the business differently, it will produce a different kind of result.

## CREATING A DIFFERENCE

There are four P's of creating a difference in business;

**1.) Packaging**

Develop the ability to transform something old into something new. Do a remodeling and make it more attractive.

There was a time I was in Dubai with my children, and we visited a playground. While we were there, a lady walked up to me to market her bottled water product. She said she was trying to launch her water business and would love to get feedback from the public. She told me all the vitamins and minerals in the water and that it would greatly enrich me.

But when I looked at the label on the bottle, there was nothing of that sort listed on it. I advised her to go back to her team, and, ensure that they listed the mineral ingredients in the water on the bottle, otherwise it would not be any different from the others.

If someone owns a restaurant where food is prepared only when ordered for, then that can be a way of rebranding that business.

If a businessman is going for a meeting to meet with reputable clients to discuss a contract worth millions of naira; if he does not own a car, he can hire one and drive himself or pay to be driven. He must also be well dressed. He must be willing to do extra to get what he wants.

A lady looking out for a husband should learn how to carry herself and walk with the proper feminine gait. She should comport herself, build herself up mentally and in other necessary areas.

## 2.) Pricing

Do not price yourself out of the market. Take your location into consideration when pricing. Every intelligent person knows that a business has its targets. The business design could target either a high, middle- or low-income earner but the target cannot be everyone.

Consider the income of the people around. Do not put a price tag that will discourage people from patronizing the business.

Pricing is intertwined with the location of the business.

If the location is not right no one will come. You may sell something good but your location may not appreciate it. Sell products that will attract the people who live in that area.

The problem is that the location of some businessmen and women today is faulty, so their pricing is faulty as well.

A jewelry seller cannot make so much from selling jewelry worth half a million naira at Igbudu market in Warri, Delta state, because of the location.

I decree and declare, that as you locate your business in the right place, you will succeed in the name of Jesus.

## 3.) Product

Integrity is the watchword here. Do not sell a product that is worth ten naira for a hundred naira. Make sure that your customers acknowledge and equate your business with quality.

Do not allow the standard and economy of the country to compromise your integrity. Do not deceive your customers.

One of the things I love about Chinese products is that they make a clear distinction between the original products and sub-standard products. Accordingly, they also allow for disparity in the price tags of the original and sub-standard products.

From today when you do business with integrity, the blessing will be yours in the name of Jesus.

*"Ye shall not steal, neither deal falsely, neither lie one to another."Leviticus 19:11.*

Do not make yourself a millionaire through deceit and cheating. Dealing with fake products and selling them at the price of genuine products is pure deceit. Although it may yield huge profits, with time, your customers will realize they are being cheated and stop patronizing your business.

**4.) Publicity**

Create awareness for the business.

If your products are hidden from the public eye, they cannot get the attention of your customers. Adequate and strategic plans must be put in place to advertise and give a wide and far reach to the products.

Advertising a business can be expensive, but it is a worthwhile investment that will eventually payback.

Most Christian brothers and sisters are unaware of what, they as individuals, do for a living. They do not market themselves or their businesses. This is wrong!

If people on the outside are aware of the business you run, those in the church should also be aware. After fasting and praying, speak to them about the business and invite them to patronize it.

Be open to people professionally and let them know what you specialize in and do for a living.

**5. Promotion**

When dealing with the issue of promotion, market segmentation should be paramount. You need to answer these questions: What is my market? Whose needs am I going to meet? These are important questions because your purpose comes from the masses. So, you segment the market based on who needs it the most.

- **Market Segmentation**

When going into market segmentation, what are the things that must be investigated?

Years back, in the early stages of Global System for Mobile (GSM) communications in Nigeria, the then Managing Director of MTN, was moving around Lagos during the December holiday period and he noticed that the city was a bit depopulated and quiet. So, he investigated and found out that those who made up a larger percentage of the population in the area he had visited were from the Eastern part of the country. They had all travelled to their home towns for the festive season. So, he got his company to install and ensure the availability of networks across the whole of the Eastern part of the country so that they would be able to reach out to their people in Lagos through his company's network.

MTN has not only expanded their outreach, but they have also ensured that both the rich and the poor can afford to patronize them. They know the rich man can afford to buy five-thousand-naira recharge cards at a go, but they also went ahead to cater to those who can only afford the hundred-naira recharge card.

They have even gone as far as allowing their customers to borrow credit or data. All of this is to ensure that they keep making money, which is the primary goal of the business.

Apart from the five P's of marketing, other strategies that can be implemented to yield success in business are:

### a) Take stock

It is necessary to take records of the day-to-day running of the business. This will position the business owner to prepare for what is to come each year.

Applying the S.W.O.T analysis technique is also key here. S.W.O.T represents the following; S- Strength, W-Weakness, O- Opportunity, T-threats.

### b) Set new goals

When you have no plans in place, it means you have planned to fail. One of the reasons why people fail to record any achievement is because they have nothing to propel them. Writing down your goals is essential.

### c) Discipline and step-by-step procedures

In wealth creation, amongst other things, discipline and habit are essential ingredients. Discipline is needed to help stay focused and for effective time management. This is because when distractions come, there are bound to be problems. But when a positive disposition is exhibited towards achieving a goal, the individual becomes unstoppable.

### d) Always be yourself

I ensure that I am authentic and truthful to myself. I never try to be someone else.

### e) Be committed and focused

How committed are you to your goal? What are you willing to sacrifice to achieve your goal? If you are indeed fully committed, motivation will follow. But many times, people strive towards motivation rather than commitment. If that is the case, it means that when problems arise, demotivation steps in and could stop that person from meeting his set goals.

People stay in marriages for years not necessarily because they are motivated but because of commitment.

### f) The obstacle is the way

Every obstacle is an opportunity to improve a certain condition.

Many times, people see obstacles as problems and run from it. But when you see it as an opportunity, it makes way for you to step into the future. So, it makes what looks insurmountable to become an easy ride.

It is in the process of solving difficult problems, overcoming frustration, and fear, that development of patience and poise will begin to unfold.

### g) Growth and comfort cannot co-exist

Growth and evolution are incubated in pain and discomfort. Some people choose comfort over pain and so continue to live mediocre lives. Abraham Maslow said, "you can either step forward into growth or backward into insecurity".

To experience true lasting success, it is important to step out of that comfort zone. You must put yourself at risk so the unusual can become the usual.

Becoming a better, smarter, richer, person, cannot be achieved while choosing comfort overgrowth.

### h) Consistency beats intensity

Be consistent in your resolve, fall seven times but rise eight times.

It is not about falling or failing but about getting up whenever you fall. It is not the individual with the best or advantageous starting position or motivation that usually wins, but the one who can last the longest. This is because despite what happens, they are the ones who will reach their goals.

**I) Choose education over entertainment**

Choosing to learn instead of being entertained is a trademark or characteristic of successful people.

Successful minds of our time are voracious readers. They invest time in their education. Some examples of such minds are Bill Gates, who reads fifty books a year, about one book per week; Warren Buffet, who reads hundreds of pages a day and is worth 3.4 billion, Helen Mosque, worth 15.2 billion dollars and who is also an avid reader.

**j) Live a grace-filled life**

Without the grace of God, nothing is achievable!

It is the undeserved favour given from one to another. It begins and ends with God.

It is very important to note that being successful requires the entire transformation of a person's life, in terms of relationships, health, career, etc. Although the change may be difficult because evolving is painful. And that is why most people do not do it. Those who have decided to give up, are those who remain on the floor.

I prophesy to you that your business will experience growth, it will expand in every direction in the name of Jesus.

### SUCCESS IN BUSINESS
## PRAYER

- Father, I ask you today to help me to succeed in my business. Teach me how to do things differently from others so that people will see me, and I will be their choice. Father, make me a success story in my business in the name of Jesus.

## CHAPTER SEVEN
# STRATEGIES TO ATTAIN SUCCESS THROUGH BIBLICAL EXAMPLES

> Grace and favour may open the door of opportunities, but soft skills are needed to retain that position and to progress.

CHAPTER SEVEN

## STRATEGIES TO ATTAIN SUCCESS THROUGH BIBLICAL EXAMPLES

In a bid to experience long-lasting success, it is necessary to be strategically positioned. The decisions made and actions taken in the previous years should not be the same for the following years. Also, the strategy that worked yesterday may not work today. It may require a little adjustment.

*"Beloveth above all things I wish for you to prosper, be in health as thy soul prospereth."*
*3 John 1:2(KJV)*

It is in the heart of God for every one of his children to succeed in life. Whose success story will I be testifying of tomorrow? Who did I write this book for? Success is coming your way in the name of Jesus.

In the Book of Esther, chapter 1, the Bible tells us about a woman named Vashti, who was a beauty to behold. The king saw her and chose her to be his queen, but she could not sustain her position because she lacked soft skills.

Grace and favour may open the door of opportunities, but soft skills are needed to retain that position and to progress.

It is scientifically proven that eighty-five percent of people that succeed in their jobs have soft skills. Some people wonder why those with first-class degrees get jobs and do not progress in the career ladder, while those with lower classes of degree climb the ladder of success. More often than not, it is all because the latter embraced and developed their soft skills.

Vashti could not handle her position. The Bible says she lost her place because she lacked something essential. If you lack anything in your life, I pray that God will supply it. The opportunity that God has opened unto you will not be wasted. The skills you need to be a success story and to stand above your equals, God will give to you, in the name of Jesus.

## ESTHER'S STRATEGY

*"So it came to pass when the king's commandment and his decree was heard, and when maidens are gathered together unto Sushan in the palace, to the custody of Hegai, that Esther was brought also unto the King's house, to the custody of Hegai, keeper of the women. And the maiden pleased him, and she obtained kindness of him; and he speedily gave her things for purification, with such things as belonged to her, and seven maidens, which were meet to*

*be given her, out of the king's palace, and he preferred her and her maids unto the best place of the house of the women. Esther had not shewed her people nor her kindred: for Mordecai had charged her that she should not shew it. And Mordecai walked everyday before the court of the women's house, to know how Esther did, and what should become of her. Now when every maid's turn was come to go into King Ahasuerus, after that she had been twelve months according to the manner of the women, (for so wherethe days of their purification accomplished, to wit, six months with oil of myrrh, and six months with sweet odours, and with other things for the purifying of the women. Then thus came every maiden unto the king; whatsoever she desired was given her to go with her out of the house of the women unto the king's house. In the evening, she went and on the morrow, she returned into the second house of the women, to the custody of Shaashgaz, the king's chamberlain, which kept the concubines: she came in unto the king no more, except the king delighted her, and that she was called by name. Now when the turn of Esther, the daughter of Abihail the uncle of Mordecai, who had taken her for his daughter, was come to go in unto the king, she required nothing but what Hegai the king's chamberlain, the keeper of the women, appointed. And Esther obtained favour in the sight of all them that looked upon her. So, Esther was taken unto the king Ahasuerus unto his house royal in the tenth month, which is the month Tebeth, in the seventh year of his reign. And the king loved Esther above all the women, and she obtained grace and favour in his sight more than all the virgins; so that he set the royal crown upon her head and made her queen instead of Vashti"* Esther 2:8-17; KJV.

When the announcement for the replacement of the queen was made, everyone showed up including Esther. When she presented herself, she did not even say a word but she had something others did not.

Others may have been more beautiful than she was, but there was something distinct about her; she carried herself with dignity and honour, she walked with gait and splendour.

When Esther met the king, as written in *Esther 2:9, "that the maiden pleased him…"* What could she have had? She was favoured amongst men.

When defending a project or a job, it is not only the content that matters, the presentation is taken into consideration as well.

The Bible says that when Esther showed up something was different; he took a liking to her.

Esther was able to stand out because she possessed skills on the inside that were noticeable, and one of which was that she had good problem-solving skills. In chapter 3, she was confronted with a problem. The Bible says Mordecai pleaded with her to save her people and herself. Initially, she refused although she gave her reasons. Later, she changed her mind and agreed to help. The Bible says not only did she fast and pray with her women, but she also deployed a strategy to help her win the heart of the king.

Many times, we concentrate more on fasting, we pray for favour and grace, believing it is all we need, unaware that it goes beyond that.

An employer will not promote an employee who only sees

the problems in the organization without proffering solutions. That kind of mindset pulls many people down the ladder of success.

There will always be challenges that will threaten the existence of an organization, but learn to hold the keys to the problems, because that was the reason the job was created. It is mandatory to be a problem solver.

The children of Israel are a good example of people who murmured a lot. Irrespective of what was done for them, it was never good enough. When there are such people in a local assembly, there will be serious trouble.

The Bible says Esther was preferred amongst men. How one presents oneself will determine how they will be treated. As children of God, it is important to remember who we carry on the inside. The Bible says *"greater is he that is in me than he that is in the world."*

In an interview when asked to speak, defend yourself with confidence and you will stand out.

Many people cannot stand tall and be fearless against all manners of intimidations because they are ignorant of who they are. It is normal for people to try to use the weak points of others to pull them down. But bear in mind that regardless of whatever they do, they are wasting their time because you have God by your side.

## ESTHER'S PROBLEM-SOLVING SKILLS

### a) She Thought Outside the Box

Esther was aware of the problem before her. She gathered

information about it and thought of a plan to solve the problem. She prayed about it and knew that she needed something extra to change the situation of her people. So, she treaded with wisdom and got the information she needed to change the face of the dice. After praying and fasting, there is a need to do some practical things just like Esther did.

To be a problem solver, you need to have adequate skills to evaluate the problem by gathering the necessary information. Do not run away from it, evaluate it, find out the kind of problem it is, and then gather the necessary required information.

### b) She Identified Solutions

Esther must have sat down to think and draw up a plan on how she was going to do things differently so she could achieve results. She needed to come up with the best solution and so she took her time to think through a solution.

Sometimes it might just be one or two options available, but the best option needs to be identified.

### c) She Understood That There was no Problem That God Cannot Solve.

What contributions do we have to make towards solving the problem? We have to study the problem, and then map out possible solutions to the problem, and then God will step in to show the right way. For instance, if a business is experiencing difficulties, the business owner should be able to work out the best solution to the problem. It could be that they need more publicity, or a different kind of connection or more experienced hired hands on deck. Once the owner has scanned through these options, he can then decide on the best option that will help provide a solution to the problem.

It is important to have an analytical mind. However, what does it mean to analyse? An analysis is a critical component of visual thinking that gives a person the ability to solve problems effectively. It provides the enablement to break complex problems into simpler and more manageable components. Thinkers with an analytical mindset are reserved and quiet, while curiosity is one of their strongest traits.

Learn to actively participate in analysing and solving problems around you. When a problem arises, remaining passive, complaining about the situation, without taking action will leave the situation the way it is. Such an attitude puts the word of God to shame. It makes it seem like there is no power in the word whereas there is.

- **She Possessed Listening Skills**

*"Now when the turn of Esther, the daughter of Abihail, the uncle of Mordecai, who had taken her for his daughter, was come to go in unto the king, she required nothing but what Haggai the king's chamberlain, the keeper of the women, appointed."*
Esther 2:15(KJV)

Esther knew that for her to make progress on the mission, she had to listen to someone more knowledgeable than she was.

The greatest challenge in the ministry is that we have people who believe they know it all when they know nothing. So, when they see someone become successful within a short time, they become jealous.

The other maidens, before they went in to meet with the king, requested for their heart desires. They were more interested in pleasing themselves than the king. But Esther listened to Haggai. She listened and followed the instructions he gave to her. This can be difficult for those who enjoy being heard but never attempt to listen to others.

Good leaders are listeners. Learn to listen. Change does not just happen; people make it happen.
Nothing will work for you until you learn to listen.

In organizations, people are not employed to please themselves but to please the employer. When the employee pleases the employer, it gives him an edge in the organization. Unfortunately, nowadays, employees enjoy being paid without adding any value to the organization.

When Esther appeared before the king, she knew what to do to make him feel good and happy. The Bible says she obtained grace and favour because she had been well prepared. For twelve months she had been preparing on how to present herself.

In *verse 17, "And the king loved Esther above all the women, and she obtained grace and favour in his sight more than all the virgins; so that he set the royal crown upon her head, and made her queen instead of Vashti."*

A person needs to have built capacity and be duly prepared for what lies ahead. Jesus said to Peter I will make you a fisher of men but follow me so that I can "make you." So, you see that it does not just happen instantly.

*"Then he that had received the five talents went and traded with*

*the same, and made them other five talents, likewise he that received two, he also gained other two. But he that received one went and dug in the earth and hid his Lord's money."*
*Matthew 25:16-18*

Ask yourself: **"What do I do when opportunities come my way?"**

The responsibility given to an employee in an organization is based on having the requisite capability. If the employee lacks this, then it is wise to get trained for it. When responsibilities are given out of emotions, it will lead to failure.

God will never engage an idle man. When God wants to give a man a job, he considers how he manages his personal life. The same zeal employed in pursuing personal dreams is the same zeal that will be used to do God's work.

The time of mediocrity is over. The time when people laze around doing nothing is gone.

Good leaders always have a vision and purpose.

To grow in a profession, or succeed in it, leadership skills are needed.

To be a good leader, **it is important to possess these traits:**
**1.) Emotional Intelligence**

Emotional intelligence is the ability to identify and manage one's emotions as well as that of others. Without it, it is difficult to go far in any occupation, company, or business. It is a trait that can be developed.

When a business owner puts up an advert looking for staff, he is not just trying to fill a space in the organization; he must have identified a need in his organization which he believes the hired personnel can help meet.

Employees or staff are not paid by the hour for showing up at work, rather they are paid for the value they add to their organization. When we make it a desire to add value wherever we find ourselves, we become sought out by others.

Emotional Intelligence is needed to achieve a purpose, for promotions and to grow from one ladder of success to another. I get tired when I hear people put all the blame on the devil. Yes, he plays a part, but there are times we need to deal with the enemy within.

Sometimes, when people lose their jobs, they are the cause of the loss and not the devil. If you cannot carry out a role, the business owner would have no choice but to lay you off. May that not be your portion.

To achieve success, there is the need to be associated with those that have people knowledge or people skills. To grow in emotional intelligence, the following three skills are necessary:

- The ability to identify and manage one's emotions as well as that of others.
- The ability to harness emotions and apply them to tasks, like thinking and problem-solving.
- The ability to manage emotions generally

**2.) Be a Good Follower**

To become a good leader, one must be a good follower. When people make themselves leaders without having prior experience of being followers, they are more prone to fail or crash in their endeavours. When a leader gives out instructions to his followers which he does not follow, he sends out wrong signals, and may not be regarded seriously as a leader anymore. You must lead by example! You must set directions and articulate goals. God will bless you with the leadership skills that you need. You will be able to make a difference, in the name of Jesus.

### 3.) Be a Team Player

To work as a team means to recognize people's talents and harness it for the growth of the organization. You will never see me decide without consulting others. What makes you an intelligent person is the ability to recognize what others have, tap into it, put it together, and mix it up with what you have for the growth of the organization.

The reason why my husband will sit and watch me preach is because he is an intelligent man. He sees in me what will make the ministry move forward. He is not afraid of what I carry, he is not intimidated by who I am or what I say. I am simply value-added personnel.

Every wife that knows her worth knows what it says *in Gen 2:18; "And the LORD God said, it is not good for man to be alone; I will make him a help meet for him."* The Bible says "meet", that is, someone that will come in, complement, and add value to the man. From today you will be an added value in the name of Jesus.

Wherever you find yourself, learn not to monopolize tasks. Learn to work with others to achieve goals and to harness more skills. When the man who buried one talent was asked why he took that action, he said it was because his boss was a wicked man. But more importantly, he said he was afraid. Do not be so intimidated that you keep others away, because you believe that their skills will expose your flaws. If you are good enough, you will show them the way. The church needs more people to do God's work. God brought people with different personalities into the church so that they can be a blessing and add value in their unique ways. From today you will begin to add value. Anything put on your way preventing you from coming close to the master, I remove the roadblock in the name of Jesus.

You cannot be a pastor and feel intimidated because your members are wealthier than you are. Instead, it should be a thing of pride because there will always be someone doing better, someone who shines more, dresses better, speaks better, and has a better education.

Fear limits a person. From today, work as a team, and harness your ideas for the growth of the ministry.
The master was happy with the servant who had five talents. His response to the servant is recorded in *verse 21; "His lord said unto him, Well done, thou good and faithful servant; thou hast been faithful over a few things, I will make thee ruler over many things: enter thou into the joy of thy Lord.*

A skilled man is one who would later enjoy the progress he has made. Your life will not be limited. You will go above yourself. You will do above yourself and you will achieve progress. You will make yourself useful in the name of Jesus.

### 4.) Be Determined to Endure Hard Times

No matter how challenging, tough or difficult a situation might be, there must be an enduring spirit within to deal with the intensity of the situation.

### 5.) Be Willing to Deny One's Self for the Sake of Others

Sacrifice is the keyword here. Putting the interest of another above oneself is what should be emulated here. For instance, leaders should not hijack a team project. Instead, they should be willing to push the strengths of their team mates first before theirs; as it is established that joint efforts of a team create better and faster accomplishments than when compared to the work of an individual.

### 6.) Be Trustworthy

Trust is priceless. It affects everything. Being trusted by others is a trait that must be possessed in a bid to go far in life and to achieve great success.

People are more inclined to trust you when you trust them. When you trust, you make people know that you believe and have confidence in them. This is indeed important for a leader.

Declare this upon your life:

I will add value at my place of work and in the church, I will not drain the strength of the church, I will position myself so squarely that I will be able to add value, I will not go around trying to tamper with my growth.

## PRAYERS

- Father show me how to get to my destination. Build-in me enough skills that will help me to climb through the ladder of success and become whom you ordained me to be, in the name of Jesus. Father bless me with favour and grace that promotes in the name of Jesus.

- I receive grace to be the choice wherever I go, whosoever I meet. When they are thinking of those to promote, I will be chosen in the name of Jesus.

- Father look on me, build in me the necessary skills that I need to achieve greatness and to prosper so that wherever I go, people will see a difference in me in the name of Jesus.
- Father from today give me access to emotional intelligence. Success is now my story; I will no longer fail. This year, the rock of ages will promote me in the name of Jesus.

## CHAPTER EIGHT

# USING WHAT YOU HAVE TO ACHIEVE SUCCESS

> Failing once does not make you a failure. It only makes you better.

CHAPTER TWO

# USING WHAT YOU HAVE TO ACHIEVE SUCCESS

**1.) Evaluate your wants and desires**

Failing once does not make you a failure. It only makes you better. Do not throw away the baton because it can still change the indices. That rod can still part the red sea. God has not permitted you to fail, so, you cannot be a failure. Go out there and be successful, in your business, your marriage, and in every area of your life.

Your wants and desires are part of what should drive and motivate you to achieve what you want and keep you on the right path to getting there. To do this:

- You must believe that what you want and desire is possible

- You must look inward and identify anything in your life

that can be an obstacle to achieving what you desire.

When you discover that there is something that needs to be changed, change it, do not give excuses, and stop complaining.

- You need the grace of God, self-determination, and hard work.

  With these three things combined, nothing will be able to stop you from succeeding in life.

## 2.) Keep an eye on your progress

Have a progress chart and monitor how you are faring. Even in your career, keep a progress chart. You may be born here but you are not from here. You are heavenly. You must make intelligent decisions to do what is needed at every point in time. Do not just allow things to happen to you; be intentional. Put your plan into action by keeping your eye on your progress. What does it mean to develop will power? It means to remain focused.

There are going to be distractions. People will try to stop you from arriving at where you ought to be. They may talk to your husband to try to get you derailed from your focus. They may talk to your wife as well. They may confront you directly and talk down on you to make you feel smaller than who you are just to get you distracted.

Stay focused, no matter what comes your way. You are going somewhere. Try not to be distracted. No one has ever been able to fault success. They may fault your journey because they have not seen the picture. But as long as you refuse to give up, to drop the baton or lose focus, at the end of the day they will search for you in the name of Jesus.

### 3.) Give thanks

You need to appreciate what you have, stop taking it for granted. There are many praying and fasting, believing God to have what you have right now. Some people wish to be like you. What you have is enough reason to give God thanks. As you thank God for the little you have, He will increase it for you.

### 4.) Learn to share with others

Learn to share whatever you have. When I was in school, our lecturers told us that any information we receive and do not utilize will die naturally. You will forget it. So, the greatest way to keep information is to dissipate it, share it, and not hoard it.

The Bible tells us about some men that were entrusted with responsibilities when their master embarked on a journey. He gave one five talents, another two, and the third one. At the end of the day for the one that refused to share, what he had was taken away from him. That is what happens when you do not share what you have. It will die in your hands. In Luke, chapter 9, Jesus gave thanks to God for the few loaves of bread and fish, then gave them to the disciples and instructed them to share.

How are you sharing your talent in the house of God? Do you not know that it is in the process of sharing what you have that God Almighty will give you your own?

It is a poverty mentality that will make people believe they must hold on to whatever they have until Jesus comes.

### 5.) Allow God to use your resources

Allow God to use what you have to be blessed by it. Peter shared his boat with Jesus, and he was able to catch an incredible amount of fish. He had gone out looking for food, and at that time he could have refused to share what he had in his boat, but he did not. And he did not regret it. You can share your time, talent, and finances.

**6.) Identify what makes you special**

Stop using other people's yardstick to judge yourself. One of the greatest challenges anyone can have is to compare themselves with others. Instead, understand the importance of other people and work with them. Also, understand that you are special. Find out what makes you special and embrace it. I pray that you will locate what makes you special and use it.

The woman of Samaria met with Jesus at the well and engaged Him in a conversation. She began to talk to Him. At the end of the day, of her own accord, she went to town and brought the city to the feet of Jesus. She used her social skills for the gospel. Never forget that you are special, you are glorious. There is something special about you.

**7.) Networking**

Learn to exchange pleasantries, give compliments, and socialize with people around you. Do not walk alone. Tell people about your business, and commit to connecting with them. Associate and mingle with people, because that is how opportunities present themselves. Do not isolate yourself.

**8.) Save.**

In Luke chapter 9, after the multitude had been fed, they saved up the remnants. Have you ever thought about why Jesus will be concerned with the remnants? Because wastage is not good. Jesus instructed his disciples to gather up the remnants because they might need it in the future. Perhaps the reason your business has not grown is because you are not saving. Do not eat up your capital, interest, and every other benefit from your business. No wise businessman or woman touches their capital. Be wise.

## HOW TO SHUT THE MOUTHS OF YOUR ENEMIES

On the journey to success, you will meet many enemies. But if you must be victorious, you must shut them up. How do you shut the mouths of your enemies?

### 1.) Make Up Your Mind to Be Successful

Jesus' enemies believed that their efforts to frustrate Him would make Him give up. But they were wrong. The first way to shut the mouth of your enemies is by making up your mind to be a success story.

### 2.) Talk to People Who Have Become Successful

Pick up the secrets and the tactics through which successful people have achieved their goals.

Do not waste your time trying to explain to people who or what you are. Success has a way of telling the story. From today, I decree and declare that you are a success story in the name of Jesus.

In Nehemiah chapter 2, Nehemiah was determined to rebuild the walls of Jerusalem.

In verse 5; "And I said to the king, if it pleases the king, and if your servant has found favour in your sight, that you send me to Judah, to the city of my fathers' graves, that I may rebuild it". He went to meet with the king because he was not happy that Judea was in ruins. The Bible says he determined in his heart to build it. It was not an easy task.

Nehemiah went to the king and the king told him to go and do what needs to be done, and so he did.

In verse 10, "When Sanballat the Horonite and Tobiah the servant, the Ammonite, heard of it, it grieved them exceedingly that there was come a man to seek the welfare of the children of Israel". The Bible says when these people heard of it, they were upset. They wondered what gave Nehemiah the courage to want to do something of such magnitude, so, they conspired against him. There are always people like that who do not want you to make it. They do not want you to be a success story and so they do everything to distract you. Every time they come around you, they say things that will discourage you. They say things that will make you drop your purpose. They make you think that the purpose is unachievable.

Lazy people only talk about people, successful people talk about success. A former first lady in America once said: "Great minds discuss ideas; small minds discuss people."

I have made up my mind to be a success. Make up your mind as well. That purpose is achievable, that dream is achievable. It may look greater than you, but you will achieve it! Nehemiah saw the huge task ahead of him, but he saw it as achievable despite what Sanballat and Tobiah thought.

In Chapter 7, the Bible makes us understand that Nehemiah was able to build the wall, I decree and declare that you will build your business, children, marriage, in the name of Jesus.

I release you into your testimony. You will become the Nehemiah of your time; the Nehemiah that set his mind to build and was able to accomplish it. You are that Nehemiah. I challenge every Sanballat and Tobiah, anyone working against your vision, your marriage, your husband, your wife in the name of Jesus. I tell them 'it is too late', in the name of Jesus. Everyone bringing confusion into your business, your life, your marriage, today I release confusion against them.I command you to escape every pit dug against you and fulfill your purpose. Good is coming out of your situation in the name of Jesus. They didnot know that you are the next testimony, the next success story. I command beauty to come out of your life in the name of Jesus.

### Indications You Are Ready for Success

You must be willing to pay the price and make the sacrifice. Sacrifice means doing something that is not convenient or doing a thing that costs you something.

Three things lead to this:

1. Conviction
2. Passion
3. Decision

You cannot decide to make a sacrifice without first being convinced, and your conviction will lead to passion.

Men do not have passion because they do not have conviction. Many people go into businesses, without being convinced that they will succeed. They do it for the fun of it or because they want to be part of the crowd. No business will run without passion. The passion is the driving force for the business, and without it, the business will eventually collapse.

### What do you need for stable success?

Stability is the strength to be strong and firm and remain focused in your endeavours.

*Isaiah 33:6 says; "And wisdom and knowledge shall be the stability of thy times, and strength of salvation: the fear of the LORD is his treasure."*

The word 'times' refers to seasons; there are different kinds of seasons; In other words, in every season of your life, if wisdom and knowledge are present, you are guaranteed to be firm and focused, but if they are absent, you will be weak, double-minded and directionless.

## PRAYER

- Father! please help me to use the resources you have blessed me with to achieve success, in Jesus name.

- Father! destroy all the plans and efforts of the enemy to stop me on my journey to success, in Jesus name.

## CHAPTER NINE

# FROM SUCCESS TO GREATNESS
### (THE PRINCIPLES OF GREATNESS)

> No one is born small.

CHAPTER TWO

# FROM SUCCESS TO GREATNESS (I)
(THE PRINCIPLES OF GREATNESS)

Most people cannot transcend from the level of success to a higher level because they are unaware of the principles that govern it. God governs everything He brought into the world by principles. Because some people do not know these principles, they are distanced from greatness.

Greatness is not limited to money; it is much more than that. It is when God gives you something that others are looking for.

Every human born of a woman is born with the potential of greatness. No one is born small.

You must know that when God gives you something no matter

how small it may be, others are in search of it. Do not try to make your greatness look like that of others because it brings jealousy and envy. It is only God that has the definition of everyone's greatness.

### The Trait Jabez Possessed

In the Book of 1 Chronicles 4:9-10, the Bible tells us of a man named Jabez whose mother passed her dilemma to him. How can a mother transfer her sorrow to her son? Some people still do so. Realize that no one can pass on what they carry spiritually if they do not have a blood connection with you.

If people outside your blood connection do the same kind of thing that Jabez's mother did, then there is someone that has a blood connection that they are using.

Jabez prayed. His first prayer point was *'that thou wouldest bless me indeed'*, where he proclaimed the blessings of God, while the second was for God to *'enlarge his coast'*.

The word 'enlarge' means to make bigger or to make great. 'Coast' is the line that separates land from the sea, in other words, he was telling God to extend his boundaries.
Jabez asked God to replace the smallness in his life with greatness.

What makes a man sorrowful? It is when he knows he can do better but is doing less than his best.
*Job 8:7; "though thy beginning was small, yet thy latter end should greatly increase".* That is the will of God for us.

I can prophesy for a good thing to happen in someone's life and it will indeed happen, but that does not mean that it is the normal pattern of God. What it means, is that God went beyond the principles, He broke the protocol and used His grace to bless that person.

**Integrity**

Despite Jabez's predicament, he possessed an outstanding trait required for greatness: "integrity"

*"And Jabez was more honourable than his brethren: and his mother called his name Jabez, saying Because I bare him with sorrow. And Jabez called on the God of Israel, saying, Oh that thou wouldest bless me indeed, and enlarge my coast, and that thine hand might be with me, and that thou wouldest keep me from evil, that it may not grieve me! And God granted him that which he requested."* 1 Chronicles 4:9-10

Jabez may have been going through challenging times, but from the scriptures, he had an outstanding trait; he was an honourable man. The word 'honourable' means a person of integrity. Integrity is when you live your life based on strong moral principles.

When you are a man or woman of integrity, you have tapped into the most important part of God's nature.

One of the key things every human wants in life is respect. People are not respected sometimes because they lack integrity. I have seen poor people who are respected, and others with lots of money that people pretend to respect. The reason is because the latter lacks integrity. You do not demand respect, you earn it. It is your character that creates respect.

*God is not a man, that he should lie; neither the son of man, that he should repent: hath he said, and shall he not do it? or hath he spoken, and shall he not make it good? Numbers 23:19*
*But let your communication be, Yea, yea; Nay, nay: for whatsoever is more than this cometh of evil. Matthew 5:37*

These scriptures show that God has integrity; He does whatsoever He says.

When you do what you say, it is integrity.

Life is like a building, and integrity is one block amongst the many blocks that makes up the foundation. It is the foundation that keeps your life.

If you do not have integrity, you will lack intensity, and if you do not have intensity, you will lack capacity, and without capacity, you become a victim of life.

Integrity is a gap that separates a good idea from God's idea.

It is only a man or woman of integrity that will follow God's idea even when it is unusual.

Integrity gives you the power to defeat failure by giving you success. If you are a man or woman of integrity, your weakness will become a strength. God will give you courage and you will rise above your equals and remove shame from your life.

A woman or man of integrity will not use his or her position in life to determine his or her destination in life; instead, they will look at their present position in life from their destination in life because God starts from the end and moves backward.

Integrity does not mean you have no-fault; it means admitting you are wrong when you are and repenting from it.

You must be predictable. People must be able to vouch for you in your absence because they know what you are capable of doing. When a man does not have integrity, he is deceptive.

The ability to live a life of integrity is a choice.

*Psalm 11:3; "If the foundations be destroyed, what can the righteous do?"*

## FROM SUCCESS TO GREATNESS (I)

How is your foundation? What are you building it on?

*John 19:26-27; When Jesus, therefore, saw his mother and the disciple standing by, whom he loved, he saith unto his mother, Woman, behold thy son! Then saith he to the disciple, Behold thy mother! And from that hour that disciple took her unto his own home."*

In obedience to Jesus' instruction, the disciple John took Jesus' mother to his house. There is no record that he ever sent her away. Jesus was leaving the world and committed his biological mother to a man that was not related to him because he could trust him. He had half brothers but he did not commit her to them. He knew that no matter the circumstance, John will never throw his mother out.

In the Book of 1 Kings 21:23-29; two important things can be deduced from the scripture:

- Ahab humbled himself, admitted he was wrong and asked for mercy

- God transferred the judgement from Ahab to his son.

I address any evil transfer from your father or mother's side, go. He is not the one who committed the offence, so leave him alone, in the name of Jesus.

Because of your integrity, God can step in and stop the devil.

**Due to your integrity, there are areas in your life where God can step in:**

- He will make His resources available to you (God's provision).

    *Psalm 78:72; "So, he fed them according to the integrity of his heart..."*

    From the scriptures, in the nation of Israel in the time of

David, there was no lack. David was a man of integrity, and that is why God named him a man after his heart. God was not looking at what David did but how he reacted to what he did; he asked God for forgiveness.

- He will give you direction (God's direction).
Direction comes through obeying instructions which then gives birth to decisions.
*Proverbs 11:3; "The integrity of the upright shall guide them…"*
*Psalm 37:23; "The steps of a good man are ordered by the LORD: and he delighteth in his way."*

A good man is a just man; a just man is someone who lives a life of integrity.

A just man is one who does not run after everything in a skirt. A just man is a man or woman who is not a slave to money.

A man or woman of integrity cannot be bought!

Who is guiding your steps? You cannot know everything about life or tomorrow, not even about the next minute. That is why you need a supernatural guide that will ensure that you do not miss your way.

Numbers 21:18; *The princes dug the well, the nobles of the people dug it, by the direction of the lawgiver, with their staves…*

Who was the lawgiver? God

Anyone who refuses to be guided is outside instruction and that person is in trouble.

Remember that:

- God can use your praise to guide your steps. Do not underestimate the power of your praise, there is power in praise.

  *Genesis 46:28;And he sent Judah before him unto Joseph, to direct his face unto Goshen; and they came into the land of Goshen.*

  From the above scripture, Jacob was about to move his family from Canaan into Egypt, and the Bible says he sent Judah to go ahead of him.

  He did not send any of his first three sons, he sent his fourth son: Judah. *Judah* means praise.

  There is a mystery behind praises that the devil cannot decode.

  When Israel went into Egypt, Judah went first. When they were returning into Canaan, Judah was also sent first. Even God said if you send Judah first, you are sure of taking the land.

  Whatever God has planned for your life, send Judah and I guarantee you will get what you are looking for, in the name of Jesus.

  Judah never fails, it always wins. Keep praising God.

  *Psalm 76:1; "In Judah is God known..."*

- He will make you the beginning of generational blessings

  *Proverbs 20:7; "The just man walketh in his integrity: his children are blessed after him."*

  Money is good and it is not a bad thing to leave behind money and properties for your children. But if you have no integrity, you will be leaving behind money and curses. If there is no integrity behind getting those things, then you will leave curses as well. But if you leave the world with your integrity intact, without leaving any money, you would have left an intangible blessing that will produce money and other blessings.

My husband once told me a story of a Christian man who was dying and gathered his children around him. He then told them that he did not have any money or properties he was leaving behind for them, except his integrity. So, his elder daughter called him a failed father because she did not understand the significance of what he was leaving behind. She was very angry and disappointed with her father. Then the father died, and their struggles began. She applied for a vacant position in a company and was invited for the interview. One of the panelists, when he realised who her father was, told her that her father recommended him for a job without asking for anything in return. So, because of her father, she was given the job.

She worked in the company for a few years and when the Managing Director of the company was retiring, she was made to take over from him, again because of what her father stood for.

- God will send your helpers

  You will never get genuine help without integrity. You will never achieve your full potential in life without help. You cannot succeed alone; someone must give you a helping hand.

  I prophesy that God will see your integrity and raise men and women to push you forward, in the name of Jesus.

God is ready to move you forward. He will use men and women to do incredible things in your life.

Man will never help you if God does not help you!
*Psalm 20:2; "Send thee help from the sanctuary..."*
God will arrange to send you helpers from the sanctuary in two ways:
o   Through your prayers.
o   By raising people right in the sanctuary

### There are five ways by which God can help us:

- God can use you to help you

In the Book of Exodus chapter 2, Moses killed an Egyptian and ran into the land of Midian. In verse 15, the Bible says he sat by a well thinking of how to get accommodation, protection, and provision. He did not know what to do, then something happened. The seven daughters of the priest of Midian came to the well to fetch water for their fathers' flock, but some shepherds who were there drove them away. In verse 17 Moses intervened and helped them.

Moses was looking for help, but God allowed him to be of help.

He forgot about his problems and decided to help others. The priest sent for Moses after hearing of how he protected and helped his daughters. That same day, he had a roof over his head. The man not only gave him his first daughter in marriage but also provided for him. All his problems were solved in one house. The house had everything he was looking for.

Whom have you helped so far? You may say, "I do not have any money", but who says that all people need to help others is money? Sometimes all they need is some encouragement.It is not every problem that money can solve. If you donot care for anyone, God will not care for you.

How are you touching people's lives?

There is no human being on earth that cannot help!

The beginning of your help is when you can help someone.

My husband told me how he once had a problem with his voice. If he stood to preach, in a few minutes, the voice would be gone and then he would start bleeding from his throat. He went to a hospital in London, and he was told he needed surgery. So, he was given an appointment to see the doctor who specializes in that area. However, before the surgery, the doctor decided to do a quick check on him, and in the process, recognized him. He introduced himself as a Nigerian who used to be in the choir.

He had followed and listened to his preaching, and he had always prayed for the opportunity to be blessed by him.

After he had examined my husband, he informed him that he did not need to go through surgery. He prescribed some drugs for him and told him that his voice will heal.

I went with my husband to an Island called Puerto Rico for a preaching engagement. We were in the pastor's office when we were informed that a woman from Miami wanted to see him. He was not in the state of mind to see anyone because he was preparing to preach. But when he was told that the woman had a message from God, he asked that they let her in.

God told her that my husband had a problem with his throat and that she had a sweet that will soothe and make it better. Immediately he took the sweet, he was better, and till date he still takes it.

We did not know anything about that woman but because my husband has always been of help to others, God sent an angel to help him.

*Psalm 41:12; "And as for me, thou uphold me in mine integrity…"*

The word upholds means to support, strengthen, and also to help.

From the beginning, God announced to humanity, that it cannot do without help. Some people have money but need help to have children. Some have children but need help to take care of the children. Some have houses but cannot sleep at night, while some can sleep but do not have a roof over their heads.

- **God will use your enemies to help you**

*Psalm 110:1; "The LORD said unto my Lord, sit thou at my right hand until I make thine enemies thy footstool".*

We always think that the word 'footstool' refers only to the thing you can rest your feet on. But do you know that if you want to sit on a high chair or a throne, you step on a footstool? So, your enemy is your stepping stone to your next level.

From the scriptures, in the Book of 1 Corinthians 2:6-10; we can deduce:

- **The Mysteries of God:**

What is a mystery? It is something or someone difficult to know, explain, or understand.

God has made your life a mystery to your enemies, you will step on them and get to your next level in the name of Jesus.

This mystery is very discernable in the encounter between David and Goliath.

David's father directed him to take food to his brothers who had gone to battle. I want you to understand that the journey was not about food but the throne. His father was not too happy that it was on him that the oil was poured.

What is Goliath? It is that problem that has no shoe size. It stretches your faith to the limit. It is a problem that cannot be hidden. It is the problem that gives you a name that God did not give to you.

Today is the beginning of the downfall of the Goliath in your life, in the name of Jesus.

The reason why David did not fight Goliath with a sword is because you do not fight a spiritual battle with physical things.

It is not about your strength but the mysteries. There are things God has mapped out for you that eyes have not seen nor ears heard. It is not about you but about the God you carry.

*Ecclesiastes 4:9; "Two are better than one; because they have a good reward for their labour."*

In other words, you can be labouring and not get a reward because there is no helper, but there will be no helper without integrity.

*In verse 10; "For if they fall, the one will lift his fellow: but woe to him that is alone when he falleth; for he hath not another to help him up."*

- God can use good people to help you

What kind of people does your life attract?

A lady had been engaged four times. All the men that came her way were the same kind. They were men who were takers, not men who add. They reduced her value, made her small.

And when they were done using her, they dumped her.

A man had been married three times, and for every new woman he married, he believed each would be better than the previous one, but he ended up marrying the same kind of woman each time.

**If you are not attracting helpers, you are attracting spoilers.**
**There are three aspects of David's life related to this:**

a.) 1 Samuel 16:16-18; Saul wanted to hire someone to work for him, and David was recommended so Saul hired him. In verse 21, David became his chief security officer. He was in charge of his armoury. In verse 23, he became Saul's chief singer and it appeared like Saul was satisfied with him.

However, in chapter 17:15, David abandoned the palace to go back to his sheep. This decision must have been caused by something.

In verse 58, Saul asked David who his father was? Was it that he did not know who David was anymore? It is either Saul had gone insane or he was just a wicked man who pretended not to know David.

Whatever it is that is attracting you into jobs where you bite your fingers will stop, in the name of Jesus.

b.) As a king, David's best friend was Ahithophel. He was his chief adviser. Surprisingly he jumped ship and hooked up with Absalom who had rebelled against his father David.

What kind of friends are attracted to you?

*Psalm 55:12-14; "For it was not an enemy that reproached me; then I could have borne it: neither was it he that hated me that did magnify himself against me; then I would have hidden from him: But it was thou, a man mine equal, my guide, and mine acquaintance. We took sweet counsel together, and walked unto the house of God in company."*

David in reference to his friend Ahithophel wondered how after all they had shared together could still go ahead and betray him the way he did.

c.) David had four sons that are mentioned in the Bible. His first son Ammon raped his first daughter. His second son Absalom killed the first son and almost killed David. His third son Adonijah attempted to take the throne while he was still alive. His fourth son Solomon ruled with wisdom, but along the line lost it and married a thousand wives. Something was wrong.

For six years David was locked in the wilderness; wilderness is a place of frustration, disappointment, loneliness, confusion.

*Exodus 14:3; "For Pharaoh will say of the children of Israel, they are entangled in the land, the wilderness hath shut them in".*

You will not be a stranger to good things, you will begin to experience good things.

*Jeremiah 31:2; "Thus saith the LORD, the people which were left of the sword found grace in the wilderness; even Israel, when I went to cause him to rest".*

From the above scripture, the word 'grace' signifies help.

*Isaiah 43:19; "Behold, I will do a new thing; now it shall spring forth; shall ye not know it? I will even make a way in the wilderness, and rivers in the desert".*

*Songs of Solomon 3:6; "Who is this that cometh out of the wilderness like pillars of smoke, perfumed with myrrh and frankincense, with all powders of the merchant?"*

## FROM SUCCESS TO GREATNESS (I)

*Songs of Solomon 8:5; "Who is this that cometh up from the wilderness, leaning upon her beloved? I raised thee under the apple tree: there thy mother brought thee forth: there she brought thee forth that bare thee."*

The above scriptures imply that there are helpers sent to those in the wilderness, that they can lean on and that can also guide them out of the wilderness.

My husband told me about a young man, an engineer, resident in Lagos who for five years roamed the streets of Lagos in search of a job without success so, he became a salesman in Alaba market in Lagos, Nigeria. He barely survived on his income as a salesman. One day, while at the market, he overheard an argument in a store next to theirs. He noticed a South Korean man in the store, and judging from the sales boy's discussion, he suspected they were planning to dupe the Korean. It got to a point when they started threatening his life. So, he called the boys out and warned them to stay off the man. He hired a taxi and took the man to the airport. He helped him to change his flight to the next available one. Before the man departed, he gave the boy his business card and told him to call him three days later. He did so, and the man asked if he could help sell his goods and the sales boy accepted. In one year, he had become very successful to the point that he owned two houses.

In *Psalm 119:141; "David said: I am small and despised; yet do not I forget thy precepts".* The word 'precepts' signifies principles. Certain principles control this life and others control greatness; even when the door is opened, some principles must be observed and followed.

**These principles are:**

**1.) Learn to give your best wherever you find yourself.**

I believe with all of my heart that I must give my best wherever I find myself. Greatness is a spirit always looking for where to reside and many in the church are candidates of greatness but have not experienced it because they do not understand the principle that governs it.

That is why some people experience greatness for only a few years, connoting that the spirit has been lifted.

I do not believe in remaining small; I must give my best wherever I find myself!

David was the smallest amongst his eight brothers. He had the smallest responsibility amongst them as well. While seven of them were soldiers in Saul's army, David was charged with taking care of their sheep.

Although he had only a few sheep to care for (1 Samuel 17:28), Irrespective of that, when his father sent him on an errand (1 Samuel 17:20), he always made arrangements for someone to stand in for him and take care of the sheep.
In verses 34-36, the Bible says, David, risked his life for the few sheep under his watch. He killed a lion and a bear and could have lost his life just because of them.

Greatness will continue to elude people who do not give their best in whatever they do. They may pray and fast for greatness, but it will pass over them daily because of their attitude towards what they do.

As a student, as a married couple, in your family, home and life, are you giving your best in what you do?

Some people refuse to take up any duties in the church.

They are ignorant of the fact that their assignment in the church affects their assignment in the world.

How the work of God is handled affects the way God deals with whatever we lay our hands to do outside the church.

Some people reason that their service would not be recognised. So, it would not be of any significance whether they showed up or not. They are ignorant of the fact that the owner of the assignment will take note of their services.

Luke 16:10; *He that is faithful in that which is least is faithful also in much; he that is unjust in the least is unjust also in much.*

God always tests us with small things, that is why you are where you are now. But where you are now is not where you are going to, it is a route to your true destination.

There are many junctions along the way in the journey of life. If you are not giving your best where you find yourself, you are the hindrance to your greatness.

You may wonder how long it will take you to put in your best before your greatness will appear. Only God can determine that. It may take a long time for some, and a shorter time for others.

When God truly believes that your best is coming out, then He will do something.

The story of David started when he was only thirteen years old. He was a very young boy yet he knew how to take care of every situation he found himself.

Some people hide under the pretense of being too young to make wise decisions, unfortunately, heaven does not recognise that assumption.

For instance, a young man maybe employed in an organization with the intention of making him a manager but he is told that he has been offered the position of a cleaner. As a result of the lowly position, he deliberately does not give as much attention to his job as he is supposed to, unaware of the fact that he was employed to become the manager.

But a man with a good heart who has all the qualifications to become a manager is employed as a cleaner, which he accepts and does it with all his heart. Six months later, he is promoted to a clerk, and he continues to do the job with all steadfastness and then two years later he is promoted to an assistant manager before he is finally promoted to become the manager.

So, because he continued to put in his best wherever he found himself, God found him ready and fit for his rightful position.

That was his place all along, but he was being tested along the way.

Greatness is a spirit, so also is failure!

**2.) Be sensitive and discerning so you can obey the instructions that come from your source (spiritual father).**
Proverbs 4:1; *hear ye children, the instruction of a father, and attend to know understanding.*

Back in the days in Israel, only three people were anointed with oil; the king, the priest, and the prophet. But in the presence of David's father and brothers, Samuel anointed David and called him king.

David's father understood spiritual things. He was aware of the fact that once oil was put on a man's head as king, he was to be honoured from then onwards. Yet, he would send David on errand, and David always obeyed.

There is no incident in the Bible that shows that David ever got angry when he was sent on an errand.

## FROM SUCCESS TO GREATNESS (I)

In the Book of Esther Chapter 4 verse 11, although Esther had a crown, she did not have the greatness that goes with the crown. For one month, she could not gain access to see the king.

Someone can look great but still lack greatness.

Her uncle convinced her to speak with the king, but before she could do so, she requested that her people join her in a fast. She did not do it grudgingly or angrily. She knew she had to go into spiritual warfare if she was to succeed. By the third day, when the king set his eyes on her, the spirit of greatness had entered her, so he raised the sceptre, indicating that she had been accepted.

The king said to Esther, "I will give you half of my kingdom," in other words he was prepared to rule the kingdom equally with her.

**I challenge whatever is challenging your greatness, in the name of Jesus.**

In Luke 5:1-6; Jesus saw two boats. He entered the one belonging to Peter and requested to use it. Peter had never met Jesus before and had also toiled all night without catching a fish. But with joy, forgetting all his pain, suffering, and fruitless labour, he agreed to Jesus' request. He sat and listened to the preaching, and when Jesus was done, He asked Peter to launch into the deep, where he caught many fishes.

Every fish that has been running from you, will begin to look for you, in the name of Jesus.

What you say, says a lot about where you are going; what you achieve and receive is mostly controlled by what you say. So, when you make confessions, you must believe it because most of the things God created, were done by words.

Your words will create what you are looking for, so just keep on confessing the same words.

3.) For every level of greatness desired, there is a corresponding level of spiritual battle to be fought.

If an exam is not taken or passed, then there would not be a promotion. It is the same thing about life.

The battle must be fought because it is a test that must be taken.

Most of the battles of life that eventually introduce people to greatness are usually fought in the valley of life. However, not all battles lead to greatness, some occur just to waste time. A valley biblically is a very low point in a man's life. This is when the devil does not hesitate to attack.

Greatness is always preceded by a battle or battles. It does not just come on its own. When there is a battle, then, it is a precursor to greatness.

There are many men and women fighting battles that cannot be explained, I prophesy that out of those battles, your greatness will manifest.

When a woman who has had frequent miscarriages, suddenly becomes pregnant, greatness has come.

When another woman who has been mocked for not being married finally gets married, greatness has come. So also, when a man who has been denied promotion for a long time gets promoted, greatness has come.

A very good example is Job. In Job chapter 1. Satan destroyed his business in less than 24hours. He was a man with many investments, but it was all destroyed, segment by segment in a day. At this point, Job was at the lowest point of his life. Eight months later he woke up with boils all over his body, his friends turned against him, and his wife out of frustration urged him to curse God and die.

In Job 3:3, he cursed the day he was born. He was at the lowest point in the valley. But then he got the revelation and said in *Job 19:25; 'I know my redeemer liveth'*, in *Job 42:2; 'I know that you can do everything'*, and so in verse 10, God turned the captivity of Job when he prayed for his friends. God gave Job twice as much as he had before. It was the valley experience that produced the double.

These kinds of battles take place in the valley of life.
*Psalm 84:5; blessed is the man whose strength is of God, in whose heart are the ways of them.* These 'ways' implies the principles of greatness.
*Verse 6; who passing through the valley of Baca make it a well.*
Baca is a place of tears, God is saying, wipe away your tears.

In the old testament days, one of the marks of greatness was owning well. Water was so scarce that, if a man owned a thousand cattle and had no well with water, he was regarded as a poor man.

Why do you think Isaac fought for his fathers' wells? Because it was a mark of greatness.

God is saying wipe your tears, defeat the devil and take your greatness because greater is He that is in you than he that is in the world.

You are going to be a wonder to your surroundings.

In 1 Samuel 17, David killed Goliath in the valley of Elah. It was Goliath that introduced him to greatness because Elah means a curse. David was not just battling with Goliath but with a curse.

In verse 15, David woke up one day, left the palace, and went back to taking care of his father's sheep.

I used to know a young man who would not stay in an organization for longer than six months. He would just leave the organizations without being sacked, and he would only let me know after he had done so. He had no problems getting jobs. When I would ask him why he left abruptly, he would not be able to answer.

David was already in the palace, but something moved him and he willingly decided to go back. No one sent for him. It was the curse.

If the devil knew that David's meeting with Goliath would introduce him to greatness, he would not have allowed it. But he did not know. He thought he was setting him up to be killed. He moved his father to send him so that he would die unaware of what God had planned for him.

4.) Understand that altars are important in the issue of greatness.

**What is an altar?**

For Gods altar, according to Genesis 28:12; it is the place where angels ascend and descend. However, an evil altar is a place where evil spirits intermingle.

An altar is a place where destinies are altered either for good or bad depending on the kind of altar. Altars can make people small, or great.

In Luke 4:8, Jesus said, "thou shall worship the Lord thy God, and him only shall thou serve". The altar where you worship will determine your values, i.e. the things that are important to you in life, and your values will determine who and how you serve.

A woman came down from a tricycle and saw the sum of fifty thousand naira that dropped from the tricycle. She picked up the money and waited there, praying and hoping that the tricycle owner will return to the same spot where she disembarked. Eventually he did, he saw the woman and asked if she had seen the money that dropped from his tricycle. She answered in the affirmative and returned the money to him. If it were some of us, we would thank God that He had blessed us with miracle money. But it is not supposed to be so.

Some will steal church money unaware that they are stealing the diseases and infirmities of the persons who gave the offering. When the repercussion begins, they would run to pastors lamenting that they have been afflicted and request for prayers.

*Matthew 25:40; Jesus said, two will be working in the field, one will be taken and the other left behind.*

Two pastors are pastoring in different branches, when a member backslides, one weeps and tries to win the soul back, while the other does not show any concern.

When Jesus said, *thou shall worship the Lord thy God*, He is talking about the altar.

In Judges 6:3, Israel sowed their seed, in verse 4, the enemy came and destroyed their substance, in verse 6, they were greatly impoverished. Why?

In verse 11, the Bible spoke of a great man called Gideon who was hiding in a cave, unaware that he was a great man, in verse 12, an angel announced to him that the Lord was with him and that he was a mighty man of valour.

But why was a great man hiding in a cave? In verse 15, Gideon said, my family is poor in Manasseh and I am the smallest in my father's house. What led to this dire circumstance? His father erected an altar to Baal. Baal was the god of thunder and his father was worshipping it on behalf of the community, and that was the origin of the problem for the entire Israelites. In verse 24, Gideon built another altar and he called it Jehovah Shalom, but the altar of Baal was still there.

This is what some people do today. They try to operate with two covenants from different sources.

In verse 25, when he finished building God's altar, God instructed him to pull down that of Baal.

In verse 26, God directed Gideon to pull down Baal's altar and build His own on that same spot. He could not share the same space with Baal if they needed their problems to come to an end. The next day after Gideon had pulled down the altar of Baal there was a commotion. The same people who attended the dedication of God's altar wanted to kill him for pulling down the altar of Baal. Fortunately, Gideon's father showed wisdom. He refused to align with the people. Rather he urged them to let Baal fight for itself. It made a lot of sense, so they agreed.

## PRAYER

- Father! in this success journey of my life, order my steps in the right direction, so that I can activate the path to my greatness.

## CHAPTER TEN

# FROM SUCCESS TO GREATNESS (II)

> It is one thing to have a vision or a lofty mission. The vision cannot be executed if the capacity is absent.

CHAPTER TEN

# FROM SUCCESS TO GREATNESS (II)

### (THE PATH TO GREATNESS THROUGH CAPACITY BUILDING)

**CAPACITY BUILDING**

Capacity Building is mistakenly assumed to be innate or in-built, but it is not. Capacity is the ability to acquire skills. It is the process of being tutored, trained, and developed to the level where there is complete trust that tasks will be completed. It is the process that prepares individuals to achieve greatness, competency, and greater heights in their endeavours.

It is one thing to have a vision or a lofty mission. The vision cannot be executed if the capacity is absent. It is the capacity, the number of skills that you have that gives you the power to achieve whatever it is you desire to achieve.

Capacity Building is the process by which individuals and organizations obtain, improve, and retain skills, knowledge, tools, equipment, and other resources needed to achieve a purpose competently and to reach greater heights or feet.

Obtaining a certificate is not enough but being able to utilize that certificate to the advancement of a society is the most important aspect of using one's abilities.

I pray that wherever you need to be great, God will make it possible, in the name of Jesus.

In the Book of Genesis 12:2; God said to Abraham; "I will make you great".

Where is that person who expects to be made great by God? Who is that person who desires to succeed? Is it you?

It is the opportunity you decide to take that will work for you. A man cannot be born great, he can only be made great.

Little David was at his father's backyard until God endowed him with the skill, he needed to kill Goliath and that changed the course of his destiny.

I declare that whatever you need that will change the course of your destiny, God will bring your way, in the name of Jesus.

I decree and declare that whatever you need to get to where you are going, you will receive it. God will use it to turn things around for you, in the name of Jesus.

In Genesis 21:8, the Bible introduces a young man named Isaac. It says, "And the child grew and was weaned: and Abraham made a great feast the same day that Isaac was weaned".

Every human on earth has a beginning which does not necessarily determine the end. If the decision to do and become better in the course of life is made, then that story can be changed. To remain at the same spot, one started with is an error. The fact that you started small, does not mean that you will end small. Some people started with a small-scale business but it does not follow that it cannot grow into a large-scale enterprise. Change your mind set and attempt to do something that will warrant a positive turnaround.

Isaac was weaned by the mother, but a time came when the mother told him it was enough. The father got tired and told him it was time for him to get married and found a wife for him. Yet he remained a loafer in his father's house. But one day, Isaac dropped his childish ways, and when the father saw the difference in him, he called for a celebration.

You might be in your twenties or teens but when are you going to stop taking milk, and grow up?

You must be daring, to be great!

Make up your mind and decide that you no longer need to be spoon-fed. Tell your self that you are going somewhere, even though you started small. You can end it big.

***I decree and declare that tomorrow, we will celebrate you.***

When Isaac decided to transit from being a child and grew into adulthood, he was celebrated. Many people allow their environment and what happened to them while growing up to affect them, but it is possible to walk out of that mentality.

Where you are going is better than where you are coming from, and in the name of Jesus, you will get there.

After Isaac went through the initial process, in Genesis

26:13; the Bible says, *"And the man waxed great, he moved forward until he became very great".*

When he had a change of mind, he waxed great, i.e. he grew, and as he continued to grow, he learnt management skills, acquired relationship skills because he decided to submit himself.

A child becomes a problem when he or she refuses to grow because then he expects the parents to do everything for him. But it does not work that way. You cannot remain stunted in life. You need to break out of that mentality and begin to see what you can do. Skills can be innate, but it can also be acquired.

On the path to greatness, you must be willing to discover the following about yourself;

**1.) Understand where you are.**

For you to do this, you must be prepared to be honest with yourself. You must be able to do personal assessments. You must be able to x-ray your business and be realistic about it. That is what it means to look at where you are now.

We make excuses for failure when things happen. We blame the occult world. The greatest challenge we have is that we believe that they have power over us, and because of that belief they begin to have power over us. And because you have shifted the blame to something else, you do not have any urge to aspire to become anything great. You only walk in fear instead of walking in faith. You do not believe that because He exists, you can achieve greatness. But if you walk in faith, then you can move forward, your destiny can never be limited and no weapon formed against you shall prosper.

## FROM SUCCESS TO GREATNESS (II)

Every power challenging the authority of God in your life, I command them to collapse in the name of Jesus.

What God has deposited on the inside of you, is more than able to take you to the next level. He is more than able to increase you. Until you declare who you are in Christ Jesus, you cannot make it.

I am not so much concerned about what is happening around you. I am more concerned about how you are reacting to it because that is what is going to take you to your next level.

It is about time you take responsibility. The people of the world are making money and we are working for them. They do not fast or pray. While all we do is to fast and pray and never lift our finger to do a thing, and we expect things to change. Grace can only be made available when you are in the workings.

Initially, Isaac was a child, that was his life. He was completely dependent on everyone else. No matter the age, whether you are in your forties or fifties if you cannot take responsibility for your actions, you are still a child. It is only when you are aware that failure or success is dependent on you, and your mind is made up never to fail in whatever you do, that you can refer to yourself as a grown-up. Otherwise, you are not growing.

When Abraham let Isaac stay with him longer than he should, it was because he considered that.

## 2.) Adopt a growth mindset:

Do not have a fixed mind. Adopt the mindset of change. I am very innovative by nature and I understand that the same thing can be represented differently.

If you are wearing a cloth forward, it can also be worn backward.

Every design on earth is someone else's mistake. Be different, be bold. I made up my mind long ago never to change for anyone, I decided to be me and improve on myself.
If you do not tend to yourself, life will pass you by. Lose that fixed mentality, things can be done differently.

You need to grow!

Be willing to learn and to unlearn. There are things you need to get rid of and let go in your mind for you to advance in life.

If you decide to let go of that fixed mindset, then you must be willing to question every process. Questions like: can I make it happen differently? Can I do it better? These questions need to be answered honestly and appropriately.

Advancing in age is natural, but I am one of those that has decided to grow gracefully because I can only live once.

### 3.) Invest in Training:

You need to train yourself. I do so myself. I do some courses to continue to improve myself. You have to continue to acquire knowledge it is extremely important.

Formal education will make you a living, but self-education will earn you a fortune.

It is important to learn to grow, do not remain where you are, do something to improve on yourself.
Always ask yourself, why should I be promoted? What is special about me? Why should I be given more responsibilities? Do not settle for the easy life where people do everything for you, life is not that way.

## FROM SUCCESS TO GREATNESS (II)

An organisation in the United Kingdom invited me, to come and run their organization in London for a salary of eighty-five thousand pounds per month plus free accommodation. When they did not hear from me, they increased the offer to one hundred thousand pounds. I did not go because I am already involved in something great. I was sought for because they saw what I carried, not because of the beautiful face but because of what was on the inside.

Put me in a desert place and I would spring a miracle. This is so because I have made up my mind to continue to grow, to continue to build capacity so I will be sought for, needed, and valued.

I decree and declare that whatever capacity you need for people to come looking for you, God will bestow upon you in the name of Jesus.

### 4.) Set clear goals and track metrics.

See how and where that business or company will be in the next five years.

Money is currency, it flows, and it is those who use it wisely that it remains with. If it is misused, it will fly.

It is not good enough to save it, invest as well. Poor people only save, but the rich invest.

Use money, so it does not use you!

People have a lot of 'begin again situations' and 'set back spirit' because they are not making the right decisions. When you refuse to succeed after being taught and prayed for, it becomes a problem.

### 5.) You need a spiritual well and a mentor to draw from:

Your spiritual well being matters to God. If your spiritual father can pastor others, then what about you? God must have brought you under him so you can draw from him.

The Bible says to honour your father and your mother, not just the father. It is a commandment with a promise, so if you only honour one, you are going nowhere.

**6.) Learn from your mistakes and do not rely on them**

It is not a big deal to fail. There is no man that has not made mistakes or failed in life, but the beauty of failure is for you to learn from the experience and move on to succeed.

You need to become better because of your mistakes, not in spite of them.

Many people make excuses for where they are now. Press forward, think about what can make your life better, think about how you can come out of that situation.

You may have prayed, but now, it is time to take a leap of faith and fail forward.

Stop lamenting about what happened in the past. People have forgotten, so recalling the experience of the past is unnecessary. Whatever happened in the past should remain in the past. Come up with something new.

In the Book of Isaiah chapter 43, the Bible says; *I will do a new thing*. My success does not depend on my past, it depends on what I can do now to achieve the success of tomorrow.

So, what if that man jilted you, it is his loss. You were not meant for him. Dust yourself up and move forward. The business did not work out, so what? Think about other things you can do, re-strategize, stop failing backward.

One of the things that helped me in life is that I confront

## FROM SUCCESS TO GREATNESS (II)

whatever I am confronted with and then I fail forward, I move forward. If you do not learn to move forward, life will beat you at it.

Note that if you are constantly failing at the same thing, then you are not growing. What you are doing is that you are expending a lot of effort trying to defend your mistakes and cover them up.

**There are two examples of people who failed forward to succeed:**

**1.) Fred Smith.** He attended Yale in 1962. He wrote a paper for an Economics class outlining the idea of a world-wide overnight package delivery service.

When his Professor saw it, he did not appreciate it. He said it was gibberish. His words to him were: "this cannot earn you anything more than a C, do not play with ideas that are not feasible". But today, Fred Smith is the owner of Fed-Ex. He failed forward.

He could have allowed the opinion of his professor to end the idea he nursed. He failed the course because he did not write what was expected. But through it all, he came out with an idea, and he started that company.

**2.) Abraham Lincoln** was the sixteenth president of the United States of America. He failed in many elective positions. He did his very best to run for all sorts of things. He went bankrupt, but at the end of the day, he became the president. It was his government that abolished the slave trade. He succeeded because he failed forward.

## PRAYER

- Father! make me great. You made Isaac great, do the same for me. Build-in me the capacity that is enough to promote me.

## CHAPTER ELEVEN

# THE SUPERNATURAL PATH TO GREATNESS

> Reach out to many, deliberately look for someone to lift.

CHAPTER ELEVEN

# THE SUPERNATURAL PATH TO GREATNESS

1.) You need grace for speed

Grace is given to a man or woman as an added advantage;
- It is also the unmerited favour of God
- It is a man supernaturally assisted to achieve greatness
- It is speed on your feet to arrive faster than others
- It is you being pictured by God not because of what you have done or will do, but by Him placing you far above those who are blessed with knowledge.

God in heaven will answer you before you pray. Before you ask, He will answer you. You will not depend on what you have but on the strength of God. When others are walking you will be running. When others are running you will be flying.

No man or woman will get to their destination of life before you. You will arrive quickly.

As the Lord heard the prayers of the servant of Abraham in Genesis chapter 24, so also, He will hear yours. As Abraham prayed and God answered him, so also God will answer you soon.

May the Lord, satisfy, and visit you early.

In Genesis chapter 4, although Abraham was waxed in age, he wanted the best for his son.
The Bible made us understand that before he was done speaking, that which he was looking for appeared.

## 2.) Be a natural giver

Do not allow anyone to compel you.

In the Book of Genesis 24:14; "And let it come to pass, that the damsel to whom I shall say, Let down thy pitcher, I pray thee, that I may drink; and she shall say, Drink, and I will give thy camels drink also: let the same be she that thou hast appointed for thy servant Isaac; and thereby shall I know that thou hast showed kindness unto my master."

The servant that will partake in the blessing of Abraham according to the prophetic word of open doors, must be someone who is a cheerful and a free-giver.

In Genesis 22:16; "And said, by myself have I sworn, saith the LORD, for because thou hast done this thing, and hast not withheld thy son, thine only son"
Reach out to many, deliberately look for someone to lift.

In verse 17; "That in blessing I will bless thee, and in multiplying I will multiply thy seed as the stars of the heaven, and as the sand which is upon the seashore; and thy seed shall possess the gate of his enemies".

Luke 6:38; "Give, and it shall be given unto you; good measure, pressed down and shaken together, and running over, shall men give into your bosom. For with the same measure that ye mete withal it shall be measured to you again."

Ecclesiastes 11:5-6; "As thou knowest not what is the way of the spirit, nor how the bones do grow in the womb of her that is with child: even so thou knowest not the works of God who maketh all. In the morning sow thy seed, and in the evening withhold not thine hand: for thou knowest not whether shall prosper, either this or that, or whether they both shall be alike good."

## 3.) Be faithful

Faithfulness means to be trustworthy, to be consistent. There are three aspects of this to focus on;

- Faithfulness in Character. Prov. 20:6; Most men will proclaim every one his goodness: but a faithful man who can find?

Charisma can take you to the top, open doors for you, and even put blessings in your hands. But it is your character that will keep you there and keep those blessings coming.

President Roosevelt, a former president of the United States told one of his servants to go and steal from one of his neighbours and the servant obliged. When he was done, Roosevelt fired him. When he was asked why he did so, he said, "if he can steal for me, then he will steal from me".

*Nehemiah 7:2; That I gave my brother Hanani, and Hananiah the ruler of the palace, charge over Jerusalem: for he was a faithful man, and feared God above many.*

Do you know what God wants to put in your hands that you cannot put?

He wants to give you that job, give you that contract, give you that money, but your character is driving God away. The name Hananiah means a gift from God. When you employ faithful people, they are gifts from God. When you marry a faithful man or woman, they are gifts from God.

When you are faithful in whatever you do, God will bless you in the works of your hands. There will be emergence of money from the east, and other areas and they will look for you, in the name of Jesus.

- Faithfulness in Responsibility.

*Numbers 12:7; My servant Moses is not so, who is faithful in all mine house.* God was testifying about Moses;

*Exodus 25:9; "According to all that I show thee, after the pattern of the tabernacle, and the pattern of all the instruments thereof, even so, shall ye make it."*

God instructed Moses to build a temple according to specific instructions. These instructions were very long and cover many chapters of the Bible.

A faithful man always finishes whatever God puts in his hands. If you are not faithful in the house of God, you will not be faithful anywhere else.

In Daniel 6; a lot of people conspired against him. Why did God do it for Daniel, in *verse 4; …forasmuch as he was faithful, neither was there any error or fault found in him.* When God discharges and acquits you, no one can convict you.

- Faithfulness in my faith in God

Only men and women who have faith in God will win the battles of life.

*Luke 18:8; I tell you that he will avenge them speedily. Nevertheless, when the Son of man cometh, shall he find faith on the earth?*

*Galatians 3:9;So, then they which be of faith are blessed with faithful Abraham.*

The Bible describes Abraham as 'the faithful Abraham'. He is the only man in the Bible that is described that way.

*Romans 4:18; Who against hope believed in hope, that he might become the father of many nations, according to that which was spoken, so shall thy seed be.*

*In verse 20: He staggered not at the promise of God through unbelief; but was strong in faith, giving glory to God*

Abraham was old when God promised to make a great nation out of him. At the age of ninety-nine, God changed his name from Abram to Abraham, meaning the father of many nations.

When God wants to bless you, He will allow the circumstances of life to bruise you first.

### 4.) Be mindful of whom you call a friend.

In the Book of Genesis chapter 24, the Bible says Abraham was getting old and he invited his best servant, and said, "servant, promise me that you will not give my son Isaac a wife from the Canaanites which thou sojourn with, but you will go to my homeland and look for a wife for my son Isaac." In verse 2, it is recorded that Abraham sent his oldest servant of his house for the mission. Why will Abraham subject his servant to that kind of errand? Being the oldest servant, Abraham must have given him different responsibilities over the years which he must have carried out satisfactorily well. He must have also been a wonderful example of a faithful man and a man of integrity. Abraham's servant clearly portrayed these traits and more in the course of his journey because he:

- Always made the purpose of his journey about his master and was determined to fulfil it.

- Consulted with God to help him succeed on the journey and make his master proud.

- Presented every gift that he was meant to give to the bride-to-be.

- Showed he was focused by demanding to leave with the bride as soon as he had settled everything with her family.

Abraham clearly knew the kind of man his servant was before he entrusted him with such a grave responsibility.

The partner whom you associate with will determine how far you will go in life.

2 Corinthians 6:14, "Be ye not unequally yoked together with unbelievers: for what fellowship hath righteousness with unrighteousness? and what communion hath light with darkness?"

Take out time to screen the people in your life. Evaluating them will let you know if you need to upgrade, downgrade, or terminate. Anyone not adding value to you does not deserve your time. Take your time and screen them because there are those you need to terminate or upgrade. Any friendship not adding value to you, any relationship that tends to kill your business, marriage, I terminate them in the name of Jesus.

Always remember that not everyone deserves to be the special guest star in the movie of your life. Because it is not everyone that can understand where you are going.

About twenty-seven years ago, I was awarded a contract worth millions of naira. I unwisely disclosed it to my friend, unknown to me that she was also interested in the same contract. She went behind me and talked them into cancelling the contract. That was how I lost millions.

Anyone that will make you lose your favour, I terminate their assignment, now, in the name of Jesus. Anyone not adding value to your life should not be at the front line of your life. Never put temporary people in the permanent place of your life, and do not remove the right people from the right place in your life.

Some people sit in a car that is not moving because they are not going anywhere. Stay with people who challenge you to challenge your mind. Stay with those who will come up with ideas of how to support your pastors, or be a blessing to your life and the house of God, not people who will discourage you from serving God, or who will take you out of the church. Every child of God that has been roaming around not knowing where to go to, I pull them back in the name of Jesus.

## MADE FOR MORE

The word 'made' means to create or to fashion out something. It means to bring something out of nothing; to bring alive what seems to have died, to call forth what seems to have been buried within to manifest.

"More" signifies greater than, it means something more than what it started from.

People may have written you off, but I prophesy to you that whatsoever it is that they say you can never have, you will have them all because you are made for more.

Just because you do not look great, does not mean God has not ordained you for greatness.

Who would have thought a woman like Sarah will give birth to a child? Hannah knew that she was made for more so she went seeking and she got it. You will get yours now, in the name of Jesus.

Just because you are not yet married, or you do not yet have a child, or have not built a house, does not mean you are not made for more.

## How to Triumph (Succeed) In Christ

*2 Corinthians 2:14; "Now thanks be unto God, which always causeth us to triumph in Christ, and maketh manifest the savour of his knowledge by us in every place."*

God's word is powerful, it heals, saves, and delivers because Jesus never changes.

From the scripture, I want to focus on the words "always', 'triumph' and 'in Christ'. Anyone can triumph but it is only in Christ that you can triumph always.

The word 'in Christ' is used thirty-five times in the new testament. Anytime you see something repeated in the scriptures, take note of it, do not take it for granted, God is telling us something.

Many things are impossible outside Christ but in Christ nothing is impossible. Anything you put your mind to do will be achievable. The devil will not be able to stop it, neither will any man be able to stop it. Your triumph is in Christ.

It is not enough to teach, read, talk, and know about Christ. For you to experience genuine salvation, you must be in Christ.

*2 Corinthians 5:17; "Therefore, if any man be in Christ, he is a new creature…"*

Someone may act or speak like a Christian or be around Christ but not in Christ. There are people in the church still carrying 'old character' around, and you wonder if they are Christians. Being in Christ is the only place you can have victories, defeat the enemy, defeat the devil always.

The enemy will always be conquered when you are in Christ!

You may have experienced challenges over a particular thing you have been pursuing, or you may have gone through hard times in trying to achieve a goal that looks like you have been defeated, God says, in Christ you will triumph, God, will turn it around in no time. He will give you victory, in the name of Jesus.

In Acts 12; Herod got a hold of James and killed him. Then, he threw Peter in jail, but Peter discovered something in Christ.

In verse 6, the Bible says, the very night Peter was to be executed,

- he fell asleep,
- they chained him with double chains unlike other prisoners

- they put him between two soldiers.

How could he fall asleep at such a time? It was because Peter found out he was in Christ. The power of God began to move and an angel walked in, caused the soldiers to fall asleep, woke Peter up, set him free, and asked him to follow him.

The gates opened, and they stepped out of the prison.

Some people are being tormented, they are bound, something is gripping them, they are in the prison of sin and disease but God will set them free.

## PRAYER

- Father! in my victorious journey of life, order my steps, so that I can transcend from a life of abundant success to a life of extraordinary greatness.

## A NOTE FROM THE AUTHOR

My book, ***You Too Can Become A Success*** basically dwells on what I always go all-out to be each day as regards to whatever I do, "being successful". I am driven with this zeal and even when I have achieved a certain level of success, I still aspire to attain more of it. Looking back in time and remembering how I was not really considered as a candidate of success, and seeing how far God has lifted me, spurred me to shed light and expose secrets that has helped me all through the years to where I am now.

In this book, I felt the need to over emphasize on hindrances to success which are clearly visible in many lives till date. With the awareness that anyone can experience it, there must be willingness to fight and defeat these obstacles which will eventually lead to success. Also, the key principles for success and greatness must be inculcated and adhered to, no matter the trials and circumstances on the path to success. You must be focused and willing to pay the price for each stage, time and season.

This book is of high regard to me, because it contains some of my real-life experiences and the strategies which I deployed to be where God has placed me today.

The art of writing has become a part of me. I have grown to realize how much of a passion it is becoming as I enjoy touching lives with the written word. I love the fact that people out there can get to see and experience this side of me through my books.

I pray that you will have testimonies to share with the world after reading, understanding, and implementing the strategies in this book.

Printed in Great Britain
by Amazon